CLIMATE CHANGE GARDENING FOR THE SOUTH

CLIMATE CHANGE GARDENING FOR THE SOUTH

Planet-Friendly
Solutions for
Thriving Gardens

→

BARBARA J. SULLIVAN

THE UNIVERSITY OF NORTH CAROLINA PRESS

CHAPEL HILL

This book was published with the assistance of the Blythe Family Fund of the University of North Carolina Press.

Designed by Lindsay Starr

Set in Quadraat Pro and Halis Rounded
by Copperline Book Services, Inc.

Manufactured in the United States of America

The University of North Carolina Press has been a
member of the Green Press Initiative since 2003.

Cover photo by the author

Library of Congress Cataloging-in-Publication Data
Names: Sullivan, Barbara J., author.
Title: Climate change gardening for the South : planet-friendly solutions
    for thriving gardens / Barbara J. Sullivan.
Description: Chapel Hill : The University of North Carolina Press, [2022] |
    Includes index.
Identifiers: LCCN 2022008957 | ISBN 9781469669670 (paper ; alk. paper) |
    ISBN 9781469669687 (ebook)
Subjects: LCSH: Gardening—Environmental aspects—Southern States—
    Popular works. | Vegetation and climate—Southern States—Popular works. |
    Climate change mitigation—Southern States—Popular works.
Classification: LCC SB454.3.E53 S85 2022 | DDC 635.0975—dc23/eng/20220322
LC record available at https://lccn.loc.gov/2022008957

THIS BOOK IS DEDICATED TO
MICHAEL, RACHEL, CHARLES,
MARTHA, AND BOBBY, AND TO
ALL OF THOSE THEY HOLD DEAR.

CONTENTS

ACKNOWLEDGMENTS

I WOULD LIKE TO THANK the following people who gave generously of their time and expertise to help bring this book into existence: Andy Wood, Rob Zapple, Lloyd Singleton, Kate Cardamone, Jimmy Pierce, Phyllis Meole, Sarah Gray Lamm, and Valerie Robertson in Wilmington, North Carolina; Sam Pearsall in Raleigh, North Carolina; Annabel Renwick in Durham, North Carolina; Lindsey Sita Mann of Sustenance Design in Atlanta, Georgia; Ginny Stibolt in Green Cove Springs, Florida; Bob Craft in Washington, D.C.; and Rachel Murchison and Lou Leonard in Pittsburgh, Pennsylvania.

CLIMATE
CHANGE
GARDENING
FOR THE
SOUTH

Introduction

Ultimately every garden is an ideology.

—Benjamin Vogt,
A New Garden Ethic

I BELIEVE THAT WE GARDEN BECAUSE, by our very natures, we are biophiles (a term coined by naturalist and writer E. O. Wilson). There's something about living things that draws us to them, whether we're looking into the eyes of our beloved cats and dogs, studying images of spiny albino crustaceans living at the bottom of the sea, or marveling at the ruffled yellow blooms of a prickly-pear cactus growing on a sandy strip of beachfront. We humans love to see all the forms life takes on our planet, and we have a fundamental desire to relate to other life-forms.

In the case of plants, there are an estimated 91 million Americans who garden for a hobby. Some of us are captivated by the dream of making a beautiful landscape. Some garden to attract songbirds, butterflies, and other wildlife. Others simply want a decent-looking, low-fuss green area to complement the house or apartment.

Personally, I've been in love with plants for over forty years, sometimes talking out loud to them and tending to them even in the pouring rain. Like many gardeners, I've tried species from all over the world, from the flamboyant red-and-yellow gloriosa lilies native to South Africa to delicate pale-pink roses originating in China. Most survived; some perished for one reason or another. But I've never lost interest in watching what plants do.

In researching this book, I've discovered a new way of seeing the garden and the gardener's role in the larger scheme of things—seeing beyond the plants to the larger picture of gardens in the web of life. Many of us who are longtime gardeners developed our likes and dislikes based on the classic British and European schools of practice, a legacy dating back to the late 1700s and continuing, in one form or another, to the present day. Garden magazines, TV shows, and websites in many cases continue to discuss beautiful gardens from this point of view. We've all been imprinted with images of the "ideal" garden.

Whether we've been trying for a formal, clipped look or a blowsy cottage garden, a subtropical paradise or a natural woodland, we've followed the gardening rules passed down to us. Constantly digging up the garden bed, fertilizing regularly, eliminating pests and weeds by whatever means necessary, cleaning up rigorously, experimenting with exotic plants by giving them all the extras they need to thrive—this has been our playbook.

But like other aspects of life on our planet, gardening is at a crossroads, and as gardeners, we're lucky enough to be able to play a positive role in how things unfold. We can't ignore the reality of a warming planet, which is becoming more and more inhospitable to the millions of species of insects, pollinators, birds, mammals, and other life-forms on earth, including humans. As gardeners, we're realizing that we don't garden for ourselves alone but for the interdependent web of nature our garden is part of. And this may mean changing how we garden in big and small ways.

Along with many others who've written on the subject, I believe climate-friendly gardening is an opportunity we can embrace. Those of us who garden in the southeastern United States can create beautiful, inspiring gardens while becoming part of the climate change solution.

Barbara Sullivan
Wilmington, North Carolina
DECEMBER 2021

A graphic reminder of tidal surge levels at Wrightsville Beach, North Carolina, from the eight hurricanes that struck between 1954 and 2018. Predictions are that hurricanes, floods, droughts, fires, and sea level rise will all increase with climate change.

CHAPTER ONE

Climate Change

The Big Picture

Global warming is no longer a philosophical threat, no longer a future threat, no longer a threat at all. It's our reality. We've changed the planet, changed it in large and fundamental ways.

—Bill McKibben,
Eaarth

THERE IS VIRTUALLY NO DISPUTE that the earth's climate is changing. And as NASA points out on its website (climate.nasa.gov), 97 percent of actively publishing climate scientists and 200 worldwide science organizations believe that it's "extremely likely" human activity is the cause. In 2014 the United Nations Intergovernmental Panel on Climate Change (www.ipcc.ch) found unequivocally that global warming is happening and that it's being caused by the accumulation of carbon dioxide (CO_2), methane, and other gases in the earth's atmosphere. These so-called greenhouse gases are generated by the burning of fossil fuels, deforestation, farming, and cement production, among other human activities.

In simple terms, the greenhouse gases absorb the sun's radiation, trapping it in the earth's atmosphere rather than allowing it to escape into space. The more this happens, the warmer the earth gets. The warming atmosphere causes more water to evaporate from the oceans; this extra moisture in the air amplifies the greenhouse effect, warming the atmosphere further.

Both the trapped radiation and the increasing temperature of the earth's atmosphere change global weather patterns. Global warming causes rising sea levels, melting polar ice caps, and retreating glaciers, not to mention increased occurrences of heat waves, floods, landslides, fires, and droughts as well as more frequent and more severe storms. For flora and fauna, global warming combined with continued human expansion into natural areas means loss of habitat and a sped-up rate of extinction. Many ecosystems are not able to adapt to these climate change stressors.

Because CO_2 in particular plays a starring role in this process, it's important to pause for a second and think about this. From now on, many of our gardening practices are going to be aimed at not making the CO_2 problem worse and doing our best to alleviate it. Every day on planet earth, when the sun sends down its radiation, some of it bounces back into space, some of it is absorbed into clouds, dust, or water, and the rest is absorbed into the surface of the earth or trapped in the atmosphere. Because CO_2 excels at absorbing radiation rather than allowing it to escape back into space, the higher the CO_2 level in the atmosphere, the higher the amount of trapped radiation and the warmer the climate. As the percentage of CO_2 increases, the effects of climate change become more severe. As gardeners, we can take simple steps to help fight this warming trend.

An important way to understand climate change and the role we as gardeners can play in mitigating it is to look at the definition of an ecosystem. An ecosystem is defined as all the plants and animals living in one area, together with things such as the minerals, water, air, sunlight, and everything else that forms an interactive web in that one particular location. Climate change brings with it alterations in the calendars of plants, birds, insects, and other wildlife, which might all normally depend on one another in the complex web of food, habitat, breeding, and protection in any given ecosystem. Once these calendars are disrupted, larval and adult food for pollinators may be unavailable, birds may migrate at a time when their expected food source isn't present, and the vegetation animals rely on for survival and reproduction may be absent. As native flora disappear, the insect populations that depend on them may be decimated, causing, in turn, the disappearance of all the fauna that rely on those insects. We can help mitigate some of these problems by following practices described later on in this book.

Insects, birds, and other creatures are appearing north or south of their normal ranges (moving poleward) and, in some cases, migrating to higher altitudes. Plants are also migrating but generally at a slower rate. Crop pests including beetles, moths, fungi, and viruses are moving as well, some to higher and some to lower latitudes.

Increasing winter temperatures and hotter summers will favor certain invasive plants, which can outcompete the natives in a particular ecosystem as they migrate into areas where they have no natural competitors, diseases, or insects to keep them in check. Similarly, pests such as gypsy moths, black vine weevils, bagworms, and mountain pine beetles will gain advantages from shifting into new territory. Severe heat and drought can favor pests such as aphids, spider mites, locusts, and whiteflies—and severe heat will stress many plants to the point that they become more vulnerable to disease and insect infestation.

Since the time of Alexander von Humboldt in the late eighteenth century, and later Charles Darwin, we've understood that all life on earth forms an interconnected and interdependent web and that human behavior has consequences. American visionaries such as John Muir and Rachel Carson sounded the alarm back in the late nineteenth and mid-twentieth centuries about human behaviors threatening the survival of natural ecosystems. More recently scientists have realized that climate change is happening much faster and with much greater destructive force than was originally predicted.

The good news is that individuals, organizations, and governments all over the planet are tackling the issue head on with mounting energy and resources. And we, as gardeners, are well situated to take steps to mitigate the effects of climate change by planting a rich, diverse array of plants to trap CO_2, foster biodiversity, and help birds, butterflies, bees, and the entire web of animal and plant life. There are dozens of steps we can take to make our gardens climate friendly, and there are simple gardening practices we can embrace that will reduce our own CO_2 footprints. In addition to the suggestions in this book, there are hundreds of online resources and supports available to help each of us become fully engaged in climate change mitigation. Joining others is a great way to expand your climate-positive impact.

Chapter 12 of this book provides resources for delving deeper into the topic of climate change and joining others who are engaged in this effort. In particular, American writers E. O. Wilson, Bill McKibben, Elizabeth Kolbert, and David Wallace-Wells write forcefully on the urgency of the problem we face, and they warn us that time is running out.

CHAPTER TWO

Climate Change in the Southeast

The biosphere does not belong to us; we belong to it. The organisms that surround us in such beautiful profusion are the product of 3.8 billion years of evolution by natural selection.

—E. O. Wilson, *Half Earth*

FOR THE PURPOSES OF THIS BOOK, the Southeast is defined as Virginia, West Virginia, Kentucky, Tennessee, North and South Carolina, Georgia, northern Florida, Alabama, Mississippi, Louisiana, eastern Texas, and Arkansas. During the last ice age, most of this southeast region remained unglaciated, thereby becoming home to many plant species that migrated south, in advance of the ice sheets. Within this large geographical area, located almost entirely within the humid subtropical climate zone, geologists recognize many different types of land formations, but for the purposes of simplicity we can use three geophysical zones: the Coastal Plain, the Piedmont, and the Mountains. Within each of these three major zones lies great diversity.

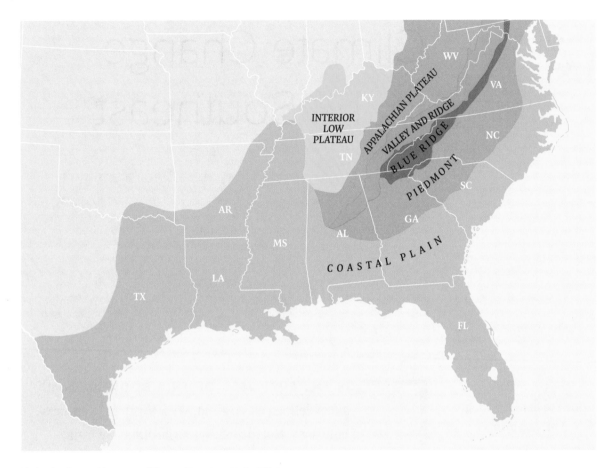

Main physiographic areas of the southeastern United States

When geologists define the **Coastal Plain**, they draw an area along the Gulf coast from eastern Texas through Louisiana, Mississippi, Alabama, and Florida and up the Atlantic coast through Georgia, the Carolinas, and Virginia, but they also include slivers of noncoastal states such as Arkansas, Tennessee, and Kentucky (running up the Mississippi corridor) because of their geological similarities. The rich diversity of the Coastal Plain habitat includes areas of well-drained sandy loam, sand dunes and maritime forests, swamps, wetlands, rivers, sounds, estuaries, bays, bayous, tidal creeks, pine savannas, hardwood forests, open meadows, and pocosins (wet, woody

The Coastal Plain is made up of beaches, maritime forests, swamps, meadows, bottomland forests, pine savannas, and other ecosystems.

areas on slightly elevated hills). Natural fires, floods, and storms cause the Coastal Plain landscape to change and shift constantly over time.

Around 25 million years ago, the waves of the Atlantic Ocean broke hundreds of miles farther west than where they do today, along what's called the fall line. This is a major geological break between the Coastal Plain and Piedmont regions, often marked by rocky bluffs and waterfalls. It's also a demarcation line that certain plants and animals don't cross. In the Carolinas, Georgia, and Virginia, parts of the fall line are marked by a discontinuous, narrow band of rolling hills topped with deep white sand, deposited along the earlier shoreline of the ocean.

The **Piedmont** includes the low, rolling hills and ridges of Virginia, the Carolinas, Georgia, and Alabama on the eastern edge of the Blue Ridge Mountains, falling away gradually to meet the Coastal Plain at the fall line. The remains of ancient mountain chains, eroded over millennia, form the Piedmont plateau. The soils tend to be less fertile and have more clay content and less organic matter than in the Mountains region. Patches of ancient rock outcroppings appear where the soil has been washed away.

The **Mountains** zone (running through parts of Georgia, Tennessee, Kentucky, the Carolinas, Virginia, and West Virginia) is perhaps the most complex of the three major southeast geological zones, composed of high and low plateau areas, a valley and ridge system, and some of the oldest mountain formations in the world, the Blue Ridge, clocking in at over 1 billion years old. The underlying granitic rock and high elevations of the Blue Ridge provide acidic soil, which tends to stay moister and cooler than the soil of the Piedmont and Coastal Plain.

The low hills, forests, and woodlands of the Interior Low Plateau region stretch from Alabama through Tennessee and Kentucky and then farther north. The Appalachian Plateau boasts sandstone canyons, steep dissected plateaus, and abundant coal bed deposits, extensively exploited through strip mining.

The Valley and Ridge region on the western edge of the Blue Ridge was created by the earth's layers folding upward and downward over 100 million years ago, exposing sedimentary rocks. Because of the richness of its biological diversity, much of this area is considered to be one of the most biologically important ecoregions in the United States.

According to the Nature Conservancy, the southern Appalachian region in general is considered to support one of the most biologically rich temperate forests in the world, including some 3,000 plant species and extensive wildlife. The temperate broadleaf forests of the southern Appalachian region are, unfortunately, among some of the most threatened habitats in the world.

Southeastern Ecoregions

Throughout the Southeast there are many different ecosystems at work. Within the Coastal Plain along the Atlantic Ocean and Gulf of Mexico, a variety of ecoregions support plants with different soil and moisture needs. Sandy beach dunes on the ocean side of the coastal barrier islands are home to salt- and drought-tolerant plants such as sea oats (*Uniola paniculata*) and bitter panic grass (*Panicum amarum*). Plants inhabiting maritime forests, situated just behind or above the dunes, must be able to tolerate high winds and salt spray. Live oak (*Quercus virginiana*) and saw palmetto (*Sabal palmetto*) are good examples.

Stretching 200 miles along the east Texas and Louisiana coasts, the Chenier Plain was formerly tallgrass prairie and marshland overlooked by elevated beach ridges, or cheniers, which supported mixed live oak–hackberry

Tidal marshes provide crucial food and habitat for fish and shellfish. They also provide a buffer against storm impact as well as nesting and shelter for migratory birds.

forests. These areas, which are important stopover points for migrating birds, have been largely cleared of the original vegetation due to residential and industrial development, sand mining, cattle grazing, agriculture, and other human activity. Remnant live oak groves, or mottes, remain important refuges for migrating birds.

The tidal floodplains of coastal rivers and sounds on both the Atlantic and Gulf coasts are home to brackish and freshwater marshes, flats, and swamps. Cypress-gum swamps, such as the Okefenokee in Georgia and Florida and the Great Dismal Swamp in North Carolina and Virginia, are populated by plants that tolerate constant water at their feet, such as bald cypress (*Taxodium distichum*) and cattails (*Typha* spp.).

The Coastal Plain zone, along the Atlantic and Gulf coasts, is also home to unique isolated wetlands such as Carolina bays, Grady ponds, citronelle ponds, and pocosins. Carolina bays support flood-tolerant trees and shrubs such as sweetgum (*Liquidambar styraciflua*) and gallberry (*Ilex coriacea*). Citronelle and Grady ponds feature plants similar to those found in cypress-gum swamps. Pocosins can be covered in dense waxy shrubs and woody vines. Poorly drained peatlands in the Coastal Plain and Piedmont support plants such as Atlantic white cedar (*Chamaecyparis thyoides*) and pond pine (*Pinus serotina*).

Along the alluvial floodplains of the Mississippi, Alabama, and Tennessee Rivers (as well as along myriad smaller rivers), floodplain forest systems have historically been home to flood-tolerant species. Once covering millions of acres, these bottomland forests have been greatly reduced in size by agriculture, drainage, and development. The rich soil created by the repeated flooding of these rivers historically formed the basis for intensive cotton growing. This in turn led to the depletion of soil nutrients and often to the abandonment of the land to succession ecosystems of grasses, pines, and other adventitious species.

Gulf coast deltas such as those formed by the Mississippi River in Louisiana or the Mobile and Tensaw Rivers in Alabama contain millions of acres of wetlands created from thousands of years of rich, sedimentary deposits. They host a variety of habitats, including fresh and saltwater marshes and wetland forests, providing important habitats for wetland wildlife.

Savannas of longleaf pine and wire grass once covered over one-third of the land in the Southeast.

Grasslands, which once covered millions of acres of the Southeast and are rich in biodiversity, have been reduced by over 90 percent since the time of the first European settlers, leaving only scattered remnants. Conservationists are at work to preserve and expand these areas. Most prominent among the southeastern grasslands were the pine savannas, found principally in the Coastal Plain and the Piedmont. Pine savannas can be wet or dry and are often dominated by longleaf pine (*Pinus palustris*) and wire grass (*Aristida stricta*). Pine savannas require fire for continued regeneration and plant diversity. Where fire hasn't occurred, or where the longleaf pines have been removed, other species such as loblolly pine (*Pinus taeda*) and hardwoods often become dominant, and plant diversity decreases markedly.

Another type of grassland, the tallgrass prairie, once had a substantial presence in the Southeast but has largely disappeared. Conservation efforts are under way in many states to preserve the remnants of this important, complex ecosystem. Prairie soils can span the spectrum from dry and rocky to wet and boggy, providing a broad range of microhabitats for plants and the animals that depend on them. In southeastern prairies, native grasses such as bluestem (*Andropogon* spp.), switch grass (*Panicum virgatum*), and Indian grass (*Sorghastrum nutans*) predominate along with a wide array of wildflowers.

Mesic (generally moist) forests occur throughout all three zones—Coastal Plain, Piedmont, and Mountains—where there is adequate soil moisture. Hickory-oak forests were originally widespread in the Piedmont and Coastal Plain, but these natural ecosystems have been greatly replaced by agriculture and pine plantations. In addition to a wide variety of hickory and oak species, these forests are home to a rich diversity of other plants. Hickory-oak forests are critical habitats for maintaining biodiversity of flora and fauna.

Considered a seriously endangered ecosystem, the Piney Woods region of the Southeast stretches from southern Oklahoma through Arkansas, Louisiana, and eastern Texas. Made up of gently rolling hills supporting pine-oak forests and seasonally flooded, wet bottomlands with hardwood forests, it's interspersed with a variety of wetlands including bayous, sloughs, marshes, and swamps. Richly diverse plants make their home in the Piney Woods, but much of the bottomland hardwood forest has been lost to human activity.

Along the Florida Panhandle, the Florida uplands are rolling red-clay hills with both hardwood and pine forests. The upland hardwood forests boast a rich array of trees and shrubs. Similar types of hardwood forest appear in the hilly uplands of Alabama, Mississippi, and Louisiana. Historically, longleaf pine and grass predominated in the upland pine forests of these Gulf coast states.

Throughout the Southeast, pine-oak forests occur both in mesic soil and in areas with drier, shallower soil. They're home to a variety of pines and oaks, many other tree species, and a diverse array of understory plants. These mixed forests can occur in Mountain areas with less fertile soil that's neither very dry nor very moist and also in the Piedmont on land where cotton farming was abandoned.

In the Mountains, sheltered moist sites give rise to cove forests where moisture-loving trees dominate. Mountain bogs and fens have many of the

Tulip poplars are among a wide variety of native trees found in mixed pine-oak forests of the Mountains and Piedmont areas and other southeastern ecosystems.

The Appalachian Mountains are one of the most biodiverse regions in the United States.

same tree species as cove forests, but their soil is deeply saturated and acidic, allowing plants such as cinnamon fern (*Osmundastrum cinnamomeum*) and swamp rose (*Rosa palustris*) to thrive.

Spruce-fir forests occur at the highest elevations in the Mountains. Red spruce (*Picea rubens*) and Fraser fir (*Abies fraseri*) co-dominate these forests. In the Valley and Ridge region of Alabama, Georgia, Tennessee, Kentucky, West Virginia, and Virginia, the dominant forests of the ridges are oak-hickory and hardwood. This region's valleys, often broad and fertile, tend to be taken over by cities, towns, industrial development, and agriculture. In a number of other places in the Southeast—such as the rocky Appalachian foothills and the red-clay hills of Mississippi—poor soil quality has made farming less practical.

By contrast, a crescent-shaped stretch of prairie land straddling central Alabama and northern Mississippi boasts some of the most fertile, moisture-retaining soil in the Southeast. Called the Black Belt or the Black

Prairie, it is now largely given over to agricultural production. Underlying this rich, black earth is a white, chalky subsoil that appears exposed at ground level in places where the topsoil has been eroded.

Climate Change in the Southeast

The overall effects of climate change on the Southeast present something of a paradox. Studies show that average summer temperatures are rising throughout the region, and warmer nighttime temperatures have seen an even sharper increase. Models show that as these trends persist, the South will be harder hit than any other region in the United States in terms of climate change's economic impacts.

This is because predictions for climate change effects—increased summer daytime and nighttime temperatures; more frequent and more severe droughts, heat waves, storms, floods, and wildfires; increased sea level rise; shorter cold seasons; increased humidity; and newly invasive plants and pests—are predicted to have a severe negative impact on the South's agricultural yields, forestry, fisheries, real estate holdings, energy costs, infrastructure, and human health.

In terms of plant extinctions, native mountain species may be hardest hit because these tend to have very specific cultural requirements and are less adaptable to change. The Piedmont and Sand Hills may see less effect from droughts, floods, and hurricanes than other areas of the Southeast, but they're still predicted to see temperature increases.

The Southeast is home to some of the most imperiled habitats in the United States and, in fact, the world. The Coastal Plain, for example, is considered a global diversity hot spot, meaning that it has such a high percentage of unique plant species found nowhere else on earth that it's deemed irreplaceable. Conservation groups in the Southeast are working across state lines to conserve endangered plant species. One of the most important organizations, the Southeastern Conservation Adaptation Strategy, brings together government agencies, businesses, nonprofits, and universities to improve the health and functioning, as well as the connectivity, of ecosystems throughout the Southeast.

Projected Change in Number of Days Over 95°F

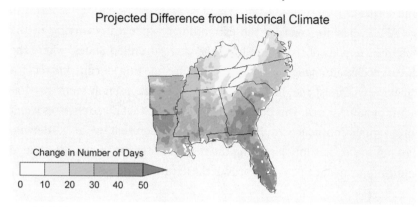

Projected Difference from Historical Climate

Change in Number of Days

0 10 20 30 40 50

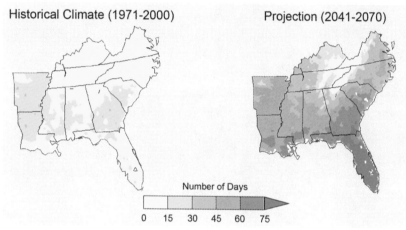

Historical Climate (1971-2000)   Projection (2041-2070)

Number of Days

0 15 30 45 60 75

Predictions for increased temperatures in the southeastern United States from the National Oceanic and Atmospheric Administration's *Third National Climate Assessment.*

Even though winters in general are getting warmer and shorter, the South occasionally experiences colder-than-usual winters and springs, with snow falling on the beaches of North Carolina and frozen iguanas falling out of trees in Florida. This seeming anomaly is related to climate change as well.

When the polar vortex (an area of low pressure and cold air circling the North Pole) expands southward from time to time, it's hemmed in by the west–east jet stream. In the past, the jet stream has stayed fairly "steady," preventing cold arctic air from reaching the southeastern United States. However, due to the warming of the arctic region, the jet stream has started to "wobble" and dip farther southward, thus giving us our colder winters and springs.

Also, when we consider the extraordinary changes occurring in the subarctic regions of the planet or in the western United States, where the effects of climate change are at their most stark (melting ice caps and record-breaking wildfires), the climate changes in the Southeast may seem less dramatic by comparison. This doesn't mean, however, that these changes won't have serious consequences. It's all the more reason that we, as gardeners, can put our efforts into lessening the negative impacts of climate change and embracing our role as stewards of the natural world.

CHAPTER THREE

The Gardener's Role

The choices we make and the rules or feelings we live by create our gardens as much as the plants that inhabit them.

—Benjamin Vogt,
A New Garden Ethic

CLIMATE CHANGE BRINGS SHIFTS that are particularly relevant to gardeners, including hotter summers, shifting plant-hardiness zones, altered timing for planting and harvesting, increases in certain pests and weeds, and destruction from severe weather events such as hurricanes, floods, fires, and droughts. As gardeners in the era of climate change, we have two main goals: adaptation and mitigation. Adaptation includes learning how and what to plant in order to have a resilient garden as well as finding ways to provide food, shelter, and habitat for our fellow fauna who are threatened by climate change. Mitigation means planting more trees to sequester carbon and cool the air, finding alternatives to gas-powered garden tools in order to reduce CO_2 emissions, and coming up with ways to source our gardening needs with a smaller carbon footprint when it comes to manufacture, packaging, and transportation.

We can become part of the solution with our climate-friendly gardens. Natives such as the Carolina lily attract bees, butterflies, and other essential pollinators.

We now understand that our gardening choices have meaning beyond our own backyard. How we plant our gardens can help slow the effects of climate change and can be of great benefit to wildlife. A garden is climate friendly if it prevents the release of more greenhouse gases than it generates and if it takes the web of life into consideration. As gardeners, we can see ourselves as stewards of the small bit of the planet that we cultivate, making conscious decisions each step of the way. Even one-tenth of an acre, when gardened wisely, can claim a significant carbon offset and benefit countless creatures. We are lucky to have a built-in role to play in combating the negative effects of climate change.

In the world of gardening, one of the leading advocates of mindful, climate-friendly gardening is Doug Tallamy, an entomology professor at the University of Delaware. In his books *Bringing Nature Home* and *Nature's Best Hope*, he warns that unless we take action now we risk losing much of our precious natural heritage. He urges gardeners to become part of the solution by creating native habitats in their own backyards. A patchwork of such habitats could, in time, form new wildlife corridors for migrating and indigenous fauna.

The new reality means that we need to change our minds, and that can be hard work. For many of us, there will be a learning curve as we open up our gardens to unpredictability rather than demanding that they look a certain way all the time. Instead of seeing dead leaves that need raking, we may see a critical overwintering habitat for garden insects. Instead of seeing spent flowers as ugly, we may recognize the seed heads as food for birds.

Rather than being in total control of what grows where in the garden, we may have to loosen up a bit and allow nature to plant some things for us. And rather than choosing plants for their novelty or easy availability, we would be better off spending a little extra time finding plants that benefit the overall ecosystem we're creating.

A sidenote: As plant and animal species migrate northward (and some westward) in the Southeast and as planting zones shift, people often ask whether it would make sense to dig up more southerly natives and bring them farther north, thus "assisting" the plants' migration and possibly helping the wildlife that depend on them. The answer, for now, is that we need to be cautious with this. Plants that spread fast could easily become overly aggressive in their new environment and outcompete existing natives. Conservation botanists are rescuing plants using assisted migration under well-researched, controlled circumstances.

Novel ecosystems are now appearing all over the United States, including the Southeast, as a result of habitat loss, human development, plant migration, and climate change. In many cases it won't be possible to restore the land to its original state. North Carolina ecologist Sam Pearsall argues that we need to understand that climate change will create more of these novel ecosystems and that we should take steps to control the process wherever we can. He suggests that we plan now for what the climate reality will be thirty years in the future by finding plants that can "adapt at speed." To find out which plants are best suited to adapt to climate change and to ensure that we reap the most ecological benefits from them, the idea is to create new experimental ecosystems in a variety of locations to see which ones are best adapted and which provide the greatest ecosystem benefits. Planners would leave natural areas intact and choose empty lots and other degraded sites for these experimental novel ecosystems.

Native sundrops attract pollinators including bees and hummingbirds and provide seeds for songbirds.

THE GARDENER'S ROLE

Native trees and shrubs are the mainstay of a climate-friendly garden. In the Mountains and Piedmont, the lovely rosebay rhododendron provides beauty in midsummer.

Basics of Climate-Friendly Gardening

Given the challenges presented by climate change—looking at it both from a practical, how-do-I-cope-with-this standpoint and with an eye toward being part of a worldwide effort to solve the problem—there are several steps we, as gardeners, can take.

1. Start with a climate-friendly garden hardscape and planting design, which incorporates all of the goals of attracting wildlife, reducing the carbon footprint, and anticipating severe weather events such as flooding, extreme heat, and drought. (See chapter 4.)

2. Choose plants and gardening practices that benefit wildlife and foster the goal of low-maintenance gardening. (See chapter 6.)

3. Use water-wise strategies to mitigate both drought and flood conditions. (See chapter 9.)

4. Respect the complex ecosystem of the soil and adopt practices that enhance rather than damage it. (See chapter 7.)

5. End the use of synthetic fertilizers, broad-spectrum pesticides, and gas-powered tools, choosing nonpolluting, wildlife-friendly alternatives instead. (See chapter 8.)

6. Eliminate or reduce the size of the lawn. (See chapter 5.)

7. Keep learning and get involved with efforts to make your community's green spaces more climate friendly. (See chapters 11 and 12.)

CHAPTER FOUR

Designing a Climate-Friendly Garden

Eventually I . . . recognized that the type of design conventional gardeners practice violates the most fundamental environmental imperative. Nothing is static in nature, every healthy landscape evolves and changes, and its plant community evolves with it at every instant of its existence.

—Larry Weaner and Thomas Christopher, *Garden Revolution*

IF YOU HAVE THE LUXURY of designing a garden from scratch, you can incorporate environmentally friendly components in every aspect of what you do. If you're working with an existing garden, there are many possibilities for upgrading the garden's environmental scorecard. Either way, there are several basic steps to any good garden design.

Get to Know Your Site

What ecoregion do you garden in? The U.S. Environmental Protection Agency has fine-tuned U.S. ecoregions into 967 separate areas, which can be viewed on the agency's "Ecoregions" page (www.epa.gov/eco-research /ecoregions). One of the primary goals of climate-friendly gardening is to determine as best we can what plant communities or assemblages occur naturally in our own ecoregion and to mimic those communities as much as possible. Check in spring, summer, and fall to see if there are any native plants naturally occurring in your site or in nearby vacant lots, roadside edges, and other neglected spots. Check in with your local native plant society, nurseries specializing in native plants, your county's agricultural extension service, or other experts near where you live, and visit nearby public gardens with native plant displays to learn not only what's native to your area but also how these plants behave in a landscape.

Once you've determined your ecoregion and what plants naturally occur there, walk around your yard and start a garden notebook, taking notes about your garden's microhabitats. Where are there high and low spots? Figure out how much sun reaches each part of the space in the morning, at midday, and in the afternoon. Observe how a "full sun" location is different in spring and in summer. Are there areas that stay wet or temporarily flooded after heavy storms?

Note which parts of the site tend to remain frost free in winter and which freeze solid. Are there areas exposed to wind? What's your soil like— sandy, full of clay, silty, rocky, or some combination of these? Take notes and keep them to refer to later. Garden author, botanist, and native plant expert Ginny Stibolt advises gardeners to "listen to the landscape."

Think about How You Would Like to Use the Space You Have

Do you want an outdoor eating area? A place for kids to play? A meditation garden? Would you like to add a water feature or a rain garden? Do you want to attract more pollinators, songbirds, butterflies, and other wildlife? Do you want to set aside an area for composting? Figuring this all out ahead of time will save having to move, uproot, or sacrifice plants that may be in the "wrong" place for how you really want to use the space.

Concentrate First on Whichever Hardscape Elements You Want to Include

Paths, a patio, arbors or arches, gates and fences, raised beds, a potting shed or potting benches, compost bins, lighting, a pond or other water feature, and irrigation—these should be laid out on paper and (ideally) installed before you begin planting. Think of paths as leading to a focal point or leading visitors to different views of the garden. Take into account existing elements such as overhead power lines and underground pipes. If you don't know where the underground utilities are, call 811.

If possible, make every element of your hardscape and planted areas serve more than one function. For example, you could create a raised vegetable garden in four quadrants with a seating area in the middle; you can grow beans on your archway, vegetables or fruit in your patio planters, and pollinator-friendly plants in your rain garden.

Choose local, permeable materials whenever possible to help absorb water and reduce pollution runoff. Locally sourced materials also use fewer carbon-heavy transportation resources. When designing your lighting scheme, look for downward-facing solar-powered options with motion detectors or automatic light timers to minimize unnecessary light during the night.

Consider building trellises or arbors for native vines such as passionflower, or maypop, which draws hummingbirds and butterflies and provides food for several larval species as well as songbirds.

Design for Low Maintenance

There's no such thing as a no-maintenance garden. Even if you're aiming to restore a native meadow or create a wildlife-friendly, 100 percent native garden, the idea isn't to just sit back and let nature take over. It will always be a question of encouraging desirable plants and getting rid of invasive and other overly aggressive plants. But you can still design and tend your garden so that it's very low on the maintenance scale.

Why low maintenance? First, less maintenance means more free time. It generally means saving money as well. And, more important from a climate-friendly point of view, the things we stop doing in the garden will eventually lead to the results we're looking for: healthier soil, the natural increase and spread of well-adapted plants to fill almost every nook, the return of wildlife, and the return of a balanced ecosystem in our small part of the earth.

The low-maintenance philosophy flies somewhat in the face of traditional horticulture, whose goal has been to cosset plants in whatever way necessary to get them to survive—even if the garden conditions are completely different from those where the plant originated.

There are a number of ways to proactively design for a lower-maintenance garden:

Low-maintenance landscaping includes using plants that thrive without the need for fertilizers, insecticides, and constant irrigation and pruning. A good example is the self-colonizing saw palmetto.

→ **When choosing trees and shrubs, avoid those likely to outgrow the space and those that will need to be constantly trimmed or pruned.**

→ **Incorporate native groundcovers to cut down on weeding.**

- → Choose native or other well-adapted plants to reduce or eliminate the need for fertilizers, fungicides, and pesticides.

- → Cut down on mowing duty by eliminating or reducing the size of your lawn.

- → Use "green mulch" and other soil-enhancement techniques to reduce the need for fertilizing. (See chapter 7.)

Design the Landscape with Four or Five Layers in Mind

The first and generally most costly items will be your evergreen and deciduous canopy trees. Configuring these trees first will help you create a framework for the next layers: smaller understory trees, evergreen and deciduous flowering shrubs, perennials, grasses, ferns, bulbs and annuals, and finally, the groundcover layer. This graduated planting scheme makes for a more attractive garden and provides greater diversity for wildlife. Thinking about your planting scheme in this way also allows you to budget for each "layer" and build the garden up as time and money permit.

The goal in choosing all of your garden layers is to create not just variety but a balance of scale so that one plant layer or one portion of the garden doesn't overpower the rest. For example, it's wise to think long and hard about the ultimate height and shape your large trees will reach at maturity before you commit to them in your design. Ideally, no one garden element would be grossly out of proportion with the others.

When mapping out transitions between wooded areas and open spaces, consider providing curved edges and alcoves to provide both sunny and shady spots to suit a variety of birds and insects. Where plant communities meet one another (e.g., where a shady area merges into a sunny area) is called the ecotone. Often this is the most diverse area biologically and is a great place to incorporate plant diversity.

Note: As you incorporate areas for native perennials into your garden scheme, think about designing these plants in larger swaths rather than as single specimens. This way you'll achieve a greater impact of color, texture, and form and also make them more apparent to birds and pollinators seeking seeds, pollen, or nectar.

Design the Garden for Natural Succession

Nature is never static, and neither are plant communities. Instead of fighting this natural law and trying to create a picture-perfect, never-changing landscape, include the slow-growing but long-lived trees that can take up their rightful amount of space once the faster-growing, short-lived plants have finished. Southern magnolia (*Magnolia grandiflora*), white oak (*Quercus alba*), American holly (*Ilex opaca*), and shagbark hickory (*Carya ovata*) are just a few examples of trees that will take some time to reach maturity but will provide rich benefits to wildlife and the environment well beyond the span of one gardener's lifetime.

Allow the garden to "plant itself" by letting some plants self-seed or spread via underground rhizomes or aboveground stolons. Using plants with a variety of reproductive strategies (setting seed; spreading by rhizomes, stolons, or suckers; dispersing spores; or creating bulb offsets) helps ensure diversity and natural succession. In some ways this requires giving up some of our control of the garden. We may have to let plants roam until they find the best-suited spot.

Because many native plants bloom for a short period of time each year, it's helpful to combine plants with different blooming seasons. A succession of blooming and fruiting will also provide greater food resources for wildlife. Note that fall-blooming perennials are often taller than their spring and summer neighbors, so consider placing them at the rear of the border.

Consider Both Variety and Repetition

Interesting gardens incorporate a variety of shapes, textures, and colors. Trees can naturally spread umbrellalike or form narrow columns; they can cascade in layers or grow into dense pyramids. Shrubs may be compact and solid, or they may spill out like fountains or be vase shaped. Ornamental grasses, palms, ferns, yuccas, and agaves each offer unique shapes to play with when incorporating variety into your design.

However, too much variety can also detract if it becomes a collection of lonely onesomes. Repetition of plant material, especially in the basic framework of trees and shrubs, lends a unifying sense to the garden so that it "reads" as a unified whole. Even an informal cottage-style garden benefits from a formal hedge or evergreen backdrop against which the looser, wilder-looking plantings can spill forth. In place of a uniform hedge, consider adding biodiversity by planting a mixed hedgerow similar to what occurs in nature.

One of the dangers of everyone using the same few, easily obtainable plants for their landscapes isn't just the aesthetic homogeneity it creates but also the reduced genetic diversity necessary for a healthy ecosystem. The limited offering of non-native landscaping plants often means higher consumption of water, fertilizer, and pesticides and the creation of narrow ecosystems more vulnerable to pests and disease.

Species diversity within your garden will make it more stable and better able to withstand harsh conditions such as hurricanes, droughts, floods, and fires. You're building in redundancy so that failure of one species won't derail the entire garden plan. You're also providing food, shelter, and habitat for many more species of beneficial insects and wildlife.

Ornamental grasses such as white-topped sedge provide textural interest as well as food and habitat for wildlife.

Group Plants

USING PLANT COMMUNITIES

In traditional gardening, we've been in the habit of combining plants without regard for their native origins. A more climate-friendly approach is to allow plants to grow in close proximity to other members of their natural plant communities. Naturally occurring plant communities are more resilient to stressors such as disease and insect damage. These groupings tend to be healthier, more drought tolerant, and more wind resistant, and they'll have long-term beneficial effects on the soil structure. Basically, these are teams of plants that have coevolved to support one another and to coexist happily. The more of these plant communities we can reproduce in our designs, the more climate friendly our gardens will be.

GROUPING PLANTS WITH SIMILAR NEEDS

Locating plants in their ideal growing conditions is a key factor in any successful garden design no matter what plants you decide to grow. Before completing your garden design, it's important to learn about the needs of each plant. Does it need full sun, part sun and part shade, or full shade? Will it thrive in dry soil, moist and well-drained soil, or soil that's constantly wet? Plants with similar needs should all be grouped together. This is one of the principles behind hydrozoning (see chapter 9) and a cornerstone of climate-friendly gardening.

GROUPING TREES

Planting trees in copses, or groups, rather than isolating them is another excellent design strategy, because as a group, they're better able to support one another against disease, insect attack, wind, drought, and other natural stressors.

Native Spring Ephemerals

Bleeding heart (*Dicentra eximia*)

Bloodroot (*Sanguinaria canadensis*)

Carolina lupine (*Thermopsis villosa*)

Clinton's lily (*Clintonia umbellulata*)

Common blue violet (*Viola sororia*)

Dutchman's-breeches (*Dicentra cucullaria*)

Dwarf crested iris (*Iris cristata*)

Eastern bluestar (*Amsonia tabernaemontana*)

Eastern columbine (*Aquilegia canadensis*)

Fire pink (*Silene virginica*)

Indian pink (*Spigelia marilandica*)

Jack-in-the-pulpit (*Arisaema triphyllum*)

Mayapple (*Podophyllum peltatum*)

Pink evening primrose (*Oenothera speciosa*)

Royal catchfly (*Silene regia*)

Shooting star (*Primula meadia*)

Spring beauty (*Claytonia virginica*)

Trillium (*Trillium* spp.)

Trout lily (*Erythronium americanum*)

Virginia bluebell (*Mertensia virginica*)

Wild hyacinth (*Camassia scilloides*)

Wood anemone (*Anemonoides quinquefolia*)

Woodland phlox (*Phlox divaricata*)

Design for All Four Seasons

Especially in the milder parts of the Southeast, color from native blooming trees, shrubs, perennials, bulbs, and groundcovers is possible twelve months of the year, and this is important for butterflies and other pollinators that may break dormancy at odd times because of warm spells in winter. It takes only a little planning to take advantage of this natural bounty.

SPRING

From late winter through the start of summer, spectacular spring-blooming native trees and shrubs add beauty to the landscape (see appendix for details). Native spring-blooming bulbs and perennials, some of which are "ephemerals," or plants whose foliage disappears into warm-weather dormancy, add beauty and diversity to the landscape.

Native to moist woodlands and floodplains, Virginia bluebells are a spring ephemeral whose deep, bell-shaped flowers attract hummingbirds, moths, and long-tongued bees. (Photo by Rachel Murchison.)

SUMMER

In all three regions, summer brings blooms from a host of beautiful native trees and shrubs (see appendix for details).

Summersweet is one of many beautiful summer-blooming native shrubs. It attracts butterflies and bees and provides seeds for birds in fall and winter.

Native Summer-Blooming Trees and Shrubs

Bigleaf magnolia (*Magnolia macrophylla*)

Bottlebrush buckeye (*Aesculus parviflora*)

Catawba rhododendron (*Rhododendron catawbiense*)

Coral bean (*Erythrina herbacea*)

Franklinia (*Franklinia alatamaha*)

Loblolly bay (*Gordonia lasianthus*)

Mountain ash (*Sorbus americana*)

Mountain laurel (*Kalmia latifolia*)

Rosebay rhododendron (*Rhododendron maximum*)

Rose mallow (*Hibiscus moscheutos*)

Silverleaf hydrangea (*Hydrangea radiata*)

Smoke tree (*Cotinus obovatus*)

Sourwood (*Oxydendrum arboreum*)

Southern catalpa (*Catalpa bignonioides*)

Summersweet (*Clethra alnifolia*)

Titi (*Cyrilla racemiflora*)

Wild hydrangea (*Hydrangea arborescens*)

Yellow buckeye (*Aesculus flava*)

Fall offers a blaze of color from the foliage of native deciduous trees and shrubs as well as from berry-laden branches that last through winter, providing important food resources for wildlife (see appendix for details).

To lengthen the season of bloom for native perennials, choose among the many fall bloomers. Some of these will grow especially tall and leggy as the summer wears on. Clipping them back in midsummer will keep them neater and still allow them to provide beautiful fall blooms.

Many native grasses are topped with interesting seed heads in the fall. Left over winter, these provide an important food source for birds.

Native Fall-Blooming Perennials

Autumn sneezeweed (*Helenium autumnale*)

Eastern doll's daisy (*Boltonia asteroides*)

Goldenrod (*Solidago* spp.)

Hardy ageratum (*Conoclinium coelestinum*)

Ironweed (*Vernonia noveboracensis*)

Joe-pye weed (*Eutrochium fistulosum*)

Maryland golden aster (*Chrysopsis mariana*)

Obedient plant (*Physostegia virginiana*)

Swamp sunflower (*Helianthus angustifolius*)

Hundreds of native trees and shrubs offer brilliant fall foliage and rich ecosystem support.

Native evergreens provide year-round beauty for southeastern landscapes. Among these are conifers, which are critical to providing nesting and cover for wildlife as well as food from seeds and needles. Some excellent native conifers that grow in all regions include eastern red cedar (*Juniperus virginiana*), loblolly pine, shortleaf pine (*Pinus echinata*), and spruce pine (*Pinus glabra*). In the higher mountain elevations Fraser fir and red spruce also provide important wildlife resources. Longleaf pine, once a dominant tree in the Piedmont and Coastal Plain, is another critical native conifer, whose natural habitats are the subject of government and nonprofit restoration efforts. Similar efforts are under way to increase and restore stands of native Atlantic white cedar, conifers that grow in poorly drained, peaty soil and that used to be plentiful along the Coastal Plain from Maine to Louisiana.

Native broadleaf evergreens often provide berries critical for songbirds and other wildlife. Examples of excellent native broadleaf evergreen trees for the Coastal Plain and Piedmont include Carolina cherry laurel (*Prunus caroliniana*), southern magnolia, sweetbay magnolia (*Magnolia virginiana*), and yaupon holly (*Ilex vomitoria*). Two other hollies, American

Planting native berry-producing trees such as eastern red cedar will provide winter food, shelter, and nesting sites for birds and small mammals. This tree is also a larval host plant for butterflies and moths.

Native Grasses with Fall and Winter Seed Heads

Bushy bluestem (*Andropogon glomeratus*)

Panic grass (*Panicum* spp.)

Pink muhly grass (*Muhlenbergia capillaris*)

Purple love grass (*Eragrostis spectabilis*)

Purple muhly grass (*Muhlenbergia sericea*)

Splitbeard bluestem (*Andropogon ternarius*)

Tufted hair grass (*Deschampsia cespitosa*)

Yellow Indian grass (*Sorghastrum nutans*)

holly and dahoon holly (*Ilex cassine*), provide evergreen resources in all regions. The Coastal Plain is host to evergreen swamp bay (*Persea palustris*), red bay (*Persea borbonia*), and stately live oak, in addition to those named above. There are also a host of excellent native evergreen shrubs (see appendix for details).

Design with the Idea of Filling In Most of the Soil with Plant Material

We know that bare soil not only risks erosion, pollutant runoff, and weed infestation but also defeats one of the main goals of climate-friendly gardening, namely carbon storage. One of the mainstays of traditional gardening has been to cover bare soil with mulch. Although mulch has its benefits (see chapter 7), our challenge is to wean ourselves off of using it in large swaths and instead adopt the more climate-friendly practice of covering bare soil with plant material.

Note: Even though covering the ground with plants is a good idea in terms of carbon storage and biodiversity, we also need to leave some patches of bare, unmulched soil for our native bees, 70 percent of whom are ground nesters. Consider building stick piles in back corners of the garden with bare soil underneath. This will help ground-nesting bees and provide habitat for birds and insects.

While you're waiting for your chosen plants to fill in the garden, consider leaving existing plants such as dandelions, clovers, and violets in place. They'll aid the soil structure, store carbon, help feed soil microorganisms, prevent erosion, and help maintain moisture and a cooler soil temperature while absorbing excess runoff and providing benefits to pollinators and other wildlife. Mulch, helpful as it is, doesn't provide this broad spectrum of ecosystem services.

A good practice is to take pictures of your desirable plants when they're still seedlings so you can learn to recognize them and not weed them out. When deciding which desirable plants you want to use to fill in the blank spaces, groundcovers come to mind right away. But there are also many shrubs, ferns, perennials, and native grasses that can expand into and take over bare spots in the garden over time.

For example, some of the colony-forming shrubs whose canopies eventually converge to provide a fairly solid mass could first be underplanted with fast-growing native groundcovers such as green-and-gold (*Chrysogonum virginianum*) or oblongleaf twinflower (*Dyschoriste oblongifolia*), rhizomatous grasses such as fringed sedge (*Carex crinita*), and spreading perennials such as lanceleaf coreopsis (*Coreopsis lanceolata*) or Maryland golden aster (*Chrysopsis mariana*), leaving no room for weeds and erosion and greatly reducing the need for mulch. Over time, these areas will be filled in by the shrubs as they spread by underground rhizomes or aboveground stolons.

Another way of increasing plant diversity is to choose plants with different types of root systems to grow alongside one another, each taking advantage of a separate soil layer. For example, you could combine deep taprooted plants such as butterfly weed (*Asclepias tuberosa*), fire pink (*Silene virginica*), or gaura (*Gaura lindheimeri*) with fibrous-rooted plants such as purple coneflower (*Echinacea purpurea*) or black-eyed Susan (*Rudbeckia fulgida*) and shallower-rooted plants such as creeping blueberry (*Vaccinium crassifolium*) or American wintergreen (*Gaultheria procumbens*).

Glossy-leaved European wild ginger and our downy-leaved relative, native wild ginger, make excellent spreading groundcovers in moist, shady areas.

Go Native

The thousands of trees, shrubs, perennials, grasses, ferns, bulbs, groundcovers, and other plants that are native to the southeastern United States have evolved over millennia to thrive in the climatic conditions in which we all live and garden. They are, by and large, much better suited than their nonnative counterparts to do battle with the diseases, insects, and climate stressors of our hot summers, hurricanes, floods, and droughts. They also support our songbirds, pollinators, and other wildlife now threatened with decimation by climate change.

If you're working with an existing garden, make it a practice to plant a native whenever you're replacing a plant that's died or outgrown its spot. Use natives when creating a new planting area in your existing garden or when you're redesigning any part of your garden.

Although filling the garden with natives suitable to your ecoregion and your growing conditions is a key practice in climate-friendly gardening, the next best step is to select those nonnatives that benefit local wildlife, are not invasive, and have been proven to thrive in your area without the need for toxic spraying and heavy fertilizing. (See chapter 6 for more information on the importance of native plants.)

Indian pink is a spring-blooming native treasure that attracts hummingbirds and other pollinators.

Consider Installing Your Garden in Phases

When deciding which plants to purchase and install first, the priority should be canopy trees, because they generally take the longest to mature and may involve the greatest financial outlay. Purchase young trees that have not been topped, because they will adapt more quickly and have a stronger form than topped trees grown for several years in a container. Also, trees grown in containers for several years before being sold have a larger climate footprint than ones that are sold after only one or two years.

Growing food promotes healthy eating, saves money, sequesters carbon, and benefits wildlife.

Next come the understory trees and shrubs. After that, it's possible to plant one or two sections of the garden at a time, minimizing the amount of work you have to do and spreading out the cost over time. Once the first areas are well established, you can move on to plant other areas. Waiting before planting the next area has an added advantage: if you enrich the soil of the unplanted areas during the waiting period by adding a layer of compost or decayed leaf mold, or by planting a temporary cover crop or wild-flower meadow, you'll be creating a rich soil biome, which will be of enormous benefit when it comes time to fill these areas with your chosen plants.

Grow Food

We can grow food in the ground, in raised beds, in containers, or on arbors and trellises year-round in many parts of the Southeast. Consider incorporating fruit trees, grapevines, a berry patch, raised vegetable beds, or other food sources in your overall design scheme. This is a win-win for your food budget, for wildlife, and for environmental health. (See chapter 10 for more information on growing food.)

Creating a richly biodiverse garden using native plants and climate-friendly gardening practices will benefit insects, pollinators, songbirds, and other fauna. The yellow-rumped warbler is among the hundreds of bird species that overwinter in the Southeast. (Photo by Robert Craft.)

CHAPTER FIVE

Attract Songbirds, Pollinators, and Other Wildlife to Your Garden

> Unless we modify the places we live, work and play to meet not only our own needs but the needs of other species as well, nearly all species of wildlife native to the United States will disappear forever.
>
> —Doug Tallamy,
> *Bringing Nature Home*

DRAGONFLIES, HUMMINGBIRDS, and painted buntings are works of art that fly by or come to rest for just long enough for us to take in their beauty. We love songbirds and butterflies, turtles and frogs, and the ballooning pink throats of the Carolina anole. But after we spend enough time in the garden, slowing down to an observer's pace, we come to appreciate the miracle of less glamorous creatures such as earthworms, moths, wasps, spiders, ants, grasshoppers, snails, beetles, and caterpillars.

Regardless of our scientific knowledge, we can all appreciate a few basic needs that all animals have. They need food, water, shelter from predators, and a place to safely bring forth the next generation, whether that's a nest in a tree or in the ground, a burrow, or the delicate foliage of a fennel plant.

The animals we're hoping to attract to our gardens, including birds, amphibians, insects, worms, and all the soil microorganisms we tend to ignore, evolved to inhabit a world full of specific species of trees, shrubs, and other plants that provide many of their essential needs. Insects may depend on young leaves of a particular plant for food. Birds, frogs, toads, and other animals in turn may depend on those insects as a food source.

This system works out well until the plants disappear. With them go the insects and the animals. Even when plants don't disappear completely, their leafing-out or flowering times may be off because of warming temperatures or fewer winter days below the temperature needed for bud break. The increase in temperature and a longer growing season are causing some spring species to flower earlier and some fall-ripening species to flower later. Wildlife has evolved to synchronize with these plant events. When that synchrony is off, insect and other animal populations can suffer and, at times, risk extinction.

According to Doug Tallamy in his book *Bringing Nature Home*, "We have taken and modified for our own use between 95 and 97 percent of all land in the lower 48 states. . . . As far as our wildlife are concerned we have shrunk the continental United States to 1/20 its original size." All of the tips and ideas presented in this book are animal friendly. Growing a sustainable, healthy garden resilient to climate change means that you'll be helping out our fellow planet dwellers as well. Here are some basic rules for attracting wildlife to the garden.

Examples of Native Larval Host Trees

American holly (*Ilex opaca*)

American hornbeam (*Carpinus caroliniana*)

American linden (*Tilia americana*)

Birch (*Betula* spp.)

Black cherry (*Prunus serotina*)

Carolina cherry laurel (*Prunus caroliniana*)

Carolina silverbell (*Halesia carolina*)

Chickasaw plum (*Prunus angustifolia*)

Dwarf huckleberry (*Gaylussacia dumosa*)

Eastern cottonwood (*Populus deltoides*)

Hawthorn (*Crataegus* spp.)

Hearts-a-bustin' (*Euonymus americanus*)

Mountain ash (*Sorbus americana*)

Oak (*Quercus* spp.)

Pawpaw (*Asimina triloba*)

Red bay (*Persea borbonia*)

Redbud (*Cercis canadensis*)

Sassafras (*Sassafras albidum*)

Serviceberry (*Amelanchier* spp.)

Southern sugar maple (*Acer barbatum*)

Southern wax myrtle (*Myrica cerifera*)

Spicebush (*Lindera benzoin*)

Sweetgum (*Liquidambar styraciflua*)

Tulip tree (*Liriodendron tulipifera*)

Viburnum (*Viburnum* spp.)

Wild plum (*Prunus americana*)

Willow (*Salix* spp.)

Examples of Native Larval Host Perennials

Black-eyed Susan (*Rudbeckia fulgida*)

Butterfly weed (*Asclepias tuberosa*)

Calico aster (*Symphyotrichum lateriflorum*)

Carolina wild petunia (*Ruellia caroliniensis*)

Downy aster (*Symphyotrichum ericoides*)

Georgia aster (*Symphyotrichum georgianum*)

Giant coneflower (*Rudbeckia maxima*)

Goldenrod (*Solidago* spp.)

Green-headed coneflower (*Rudbeckia laciniata*)

Joe-pye weed (*Eutrochium fistulosum*)

Maryland golden aster (*Chrysopsis mariana*)

Mountain mint (*Pycnanthemum* spp.)

New England aster (*Symphyotrichum novae-angliae*)

Pale purple coneflower (*Echinacea pallida*)

Purple coneflower (*Echinacea purpurea*)

Scarlet bee balm (*Monarda didyma*)

Smooth blue aster (*Symphyotrichum laeve*)

Swamp milkweed (*Asclepias incarnata*)

Swamp sunflower (*Helianthus angustifolius*)

Violet (*Viola* spp.)

Woodland sunflower (*Helianthus divaricatus*)

Mix It Up

Depending on the species, birds require a variety of habitats including grasslands, woodlands, or the dense cover of shrubs. Incorporate as many of these types of habitat as you can.

Use a variety of plants. Include trees, shrubs, ornamental grasses, groundcovers, ferns, and perennials. Use large groupings of each type of native perennial flower to make them easier for pollinators to find.

Provide a variety of flower forms for pollinators to choose from: flowers such as asters made up of ray and disk florets, spherical or tubular flowers, or flowers in the shape of funnels, saucers, trumpets, or bells. If you also incorporate different bloom times you can accommodate pollinators who arrive early or late because of climate change.

Include Food for Pollinator Larvae (i.e., Caterpillars)

If there's no larval food in the garden, there's no support for butterfly and moth reproduction. Female butterflies will fly many miles to find an appropriate host plant to lay their eggs on. Plant native, caterpillar-friendly trees, shrubs, and perennials as well as native grasses and vines.

An eastern black swallowtail caterpillar feasts on parsley leaves. Other herbs such as dill, fennel, borage, and angelica are excellent larval hosts for butterflies and moths.

Larval food for butterflies and moths is also provided by herbs, legumes, and fruits such as alfalfa, angelica, blueberries, borage, clover, dill, fennel, lovage, parsley, raspberries, and rue.

Include Food for Native Insects

Somewhere between 75 and 95 percent of flowering plants need insect pollinators in order to create the next generation. Butterflies, bees, and moths need nectar or pollen from flowering plants as a basic food source. Birds rely on insects for feeding their young. Loss of native plants, loss of native insects, and diminished bird populations unfortunately go hand in hand. And this doesn't even touch on the subject of food production for humans, which relies on animal pollinators to an enormous degree.

Native trees, shrubs, vines, perennials, and bulbs provide the pollen and nectar, leaves, and other food sources that native insects depend on. Planting these in abundance nourishes the entire food web.

Include Food for Migrating and Breeding Birds

In addition to eating insects in their native range, birds rely on berries, seeds, fruits, and nuts from native plants, especially in winter.

The prolific summer blossoms of native sourwood tree are visited by bees and butterflies. The tree provides nesting and shelter for wildlife.

Examples of Native Berry- or Fruit-Producing Plants

American beautyberry (*Callicarpa americana*)

American holly (*Ilex opaca*)

Arrowwood viburnum (*Viburnum dentatum*)

Black chokeberry (*Aronia melanocarpa*)

Blackgum (*Nyssa sylvatica*)

Blackhaw viburnum (*Viburnum prunifolium*)

Black raspberry (*Rubus occidentalis*)

Carolina buckthorn (*Frangula caroliniana*)

Carolina silverbell (*Halesia carolina*)

Chickasaw plum (*Prunus angustifolia*)

Coralberry (*Symphoricarpos orbiculatus*)

Cucumber magnolia (*Magnolia acuminata*)

Dwarf huckleberry (*Gaylussacia dumosa*)

Elderberry (*Sambucus canadensis*)

Flowering dogwood (*Cornus florida*)

Green hawthorn (*Crataegus viridis*)

Highbush blueberry (*Vaccinium corymbosum*)

Inkberry (*Ilex glabra*)

Lowbush blueberry (*Vaccinium pallidum*)

Maypop vine (*Passiflora incarnata*)

Mountain ash (*Sorbus americana*)

Pagoda dogwood (*Cornus alternifolia*)

Partridgeberry (*Mitchella repens*)

Pignut hickory (*Carya glabra*)

Possumhaw (*Ilex decidua*)

Purpleleaf sand cherry (*Prunus × cistena*)

Red chokeberry (*Aronia arbutifolia*)

Sassafras (*Sassafras albidum*)

Serviceberry (*Amelanchier spp.*)

Southern crabapple (*Malus angustifolia*)

Southern wax myrtle (*Myrica cerifera*)

Sparkleberry (*Vaccinium arboreum*)

Spicebush (*Lindera benzoin*)

Wild plum (*Prunus americana*)

Winged sumac (*Rhus copallinum*)

Winterberry holly (*Ilex verticillata*)

Yaupon holly (*Ilex vomitoria*)

Yellow buckeye (*Aesculus flava*)

American beautyberry is a native deciduous shrub that produces striking purple berries in the fall. These often last into winter, providing food for songbirds and small mammals.

Examples of Native Nut-Producing Trees for Wildlife

Allegheny chinquapin (*Castanea pumila*)

American beech (*Fagus grandifolia*)

American hazelnut (*Corylus americana*)

Black walnut (*Juglans nigra*)

Hickory (*Carya* spp.)

Oak (*Quercus* spp.)

Examples of Native Seed-Bearing Trees and Shrubs for Wildlife

American sycamore (*Platanus occidentalis*)

Birch (*Betula* spp.)

Eastern hemlock (*Tsuga canadensis*)

Hearts-a-bustin' (*Euonymus americanus*)

Pine (*Pinus* spp.)

Southern magnolia (*Magnolia grandiflora*)

Spruce (*Picea* spp.)

Wild hydrangea (*Hydrangea arborescens*)

Use Native Evergreen Conifers

Native eastern red cedar, eastern and Carolina hemlock (*Tsuga canadensis* and *T. caroliniana*), red spruce, and a variety of pines provide excellent nesting and thermal cover for birds as well as shelter for deer, grouse, wild turkey, and other animals. Birds and other animals feed on seeds from the cones; rabbits and squirrels may browse the foliage. Native evergreen conifers also host insects—an additional food source for birds and other wildlife.

Don't Use Herbicides, Pesticides, Fungicides, or Other Toxic Chemicals

Toxic chemicals will contaminate the food sources for insects and other fauna and often kill beneficial pollinators indiscriminately. Systemic insecticides are especially deadly, as they're absorbed into every part of the plant and can be present in pollen and nectar (see chapter 8).

Provide Thickets for Birds

Colonizing (clonal) shrubs can form impenetrable thickets, undisturbed areas for nesting, hibernation, and foraging that provide valuable habitat and shelter for songbirds and small mammals.

Facing page:
Native buttonbush is a colonizing shrub that attracts hummingbirds, bees, butterflies, songbirds, and waterfowl.

Native Colonizing Shrubs

Allegheny chinquapin (*Castanea pumila*)

Blackberry (*Rubus* spp.)

Black chokeberry (*Aronia melanocarpa*)

Bottlebrush buckeye (*Aesculus parviflora*)

Buttonbush (*Cephalanthus occidentalis*)

Catawba rhododendron (*Rhododendron catawbiense*)

Coastal witch alder (*Fothergilla gardenii*)

Coralberry (*Symphoricarpos orbiculatus*)

Elderberry (*Sambucus canadensis*)

Florida anise tree (*Illicium floridanum*)

Fragrant sumac (*Rhus aromatica*)

Indigo bush (*Amorpha fruticosa*)

Inkberry (*Ilex glabra*)

Lowbush blueberry (*Vaccinium angustifolium*)

Needle palm (*Rhapidophyllum hystrix*)

Oakleaf hydrangea (*Hydrangea quercifolia*)

Pinxter bloom azalea (*Rhododendron periclymenoides*)

Raspberry (*Rubus* spp.)

Red chokeberry (*Aronia arbutifolia*)

Saw palmetto (*Serenoa repens*)

Shining fetterbush (*Lyonia lucida*)

Southern bush honeysuckle (*Diervilla sessilifolia*)

Southern wax myrtle (*Myrica cerifera*)

Staghorn sumac (*Rhus typhina*)

Summersweet (*Clethra alnifolia*)

Swamp azalea (*Rhododendron viscosum*)

Sweet azalea (*Rhododendron arborescens*)

Sweetbay magnolia (*Magnolia virginiana*)

Sweet fern (*Comptonia peregrina*)

Sweetshrub (*Calycanthus floridus*)

Virginia sweet spire (*Itea virginica*)

Wild hydrangea (*Hydrangea arborescens*)

Wild plum (*Prunus americana*)

Winterberry holly (*Ilex verticillata*)

Consider Leaving a "Snag"

A snag is all or part of a dead tree, which can provide food for insects, in turn providing food for birds and small mammals. A snag can also shelter amphibians, reptiles, and mammals and act as a nesting place for birds. As it decays, it enriches the soil and creates its own microclimate where a diverse variety of plants can take root.

Leave Seed Heads to Dry

Leaving seed heads to dry on the plant in the fall and to persist over winter provides valuable food for birds when other food sources may be scarce. Excellent seed sources for birds include all the native grasses as well as numerous perennials and vines.

Native Perennials with Fall and Winter Seed Heads

Beach blanketflower (*Gaillardia pulchella*)

Black-eyed Susan (*Rudbeckia fulgida*)

Butterfly weed (*Asclepias tuberosa*)

Coneflower (*Echinacea* spp.)

Coreopsis (*Coreopsis* spp.)

Cup plant (*Silphium perfoliatum*)

Goldenrod (*Solidago* spp.)

Ironweed (*Vernonia noveboracensis*)

Joe-pye weed (*Eutrochium fistulosum*)

Sundrops (*Oenothera fruticosa*)

Swamp sunflower (*Helianthus angustifolius*)

Consider the Pollinators and Beneficial Insects during Fall and Spring Cleanup

Butterflies, bees, and other pollinators as well as beneficial insects such as lacewings, ladybugs, and parasitic wasps overwinter in leaf litter or in the dry, hollow stalks of perennials. Postponing your fall cleanup until the following spring preserves their valuable habitat. In the spring, wait until the temperature is above fifty degrees for at least seven days before starting your cleanup. Depending on the species, insects need warm weather or longer day length to break out of their winter dormancy. When you do cut down the dried stalks, consider bundling them and leaving them in an out-of-the-way spot to allow the overwintering insects to emerge. In spring, wait for warmer weather before putting down a layer of mulch, giving ground-burrowing insects a chance to emerge.

Provide a Water Source for Birds and Butterflies

A water source can be as elaborate as a pond or solar-powered fountain or as simple as a dish. If it's installed near a thicket of shrubs or trees, this will give the birds cover as an added bonus, but the National Wildlife Federation recommends placing feeders and birdbaths at least ten to twelve feet away from any potential hiding places for cats. A recirculating pond/stream combination will attract birds, butterflies, dragonflies, turtles, frogs, and other creatures.

Find Ways to Make Planting Corridors

By connecting fragmented natural areas, we can give wildlife paths to travel and native plants ground to seed themselves. In addition to working in your own garden, consider working with neighbors or with community organizations to create wildlife corridors via a series of connected or nearby gardens.

Reconsider the Ubiquitous American Lawn

Possibly the number one step we could all take to cut back on maintenance and benefit Mother Nature would be to reduce or eliminate our lawns. Lawns occupy over 40 million acres, or 63,000 square miles, of land in the

Facing page:
Leaving seed heads on plants over the winter provides food for birds and other animals. After its bright blue flowers finish blooming, climbing aster is smothered in fluffy seedpods.

continental United States. This includes parks, athletic fields, schools, and golf courses, as well as lawns attached to homes. It's hard to imagine suburban America without seeing lawns.

This widespread love of uniformly mowed green spaces can be traced back to eighteenth-century England, when the landscape architect Capability Brown tapped into the spirit of the times. In response to the increase in industrialization and urbanization came a nostalgia for a romanticized, idyllic rural past where life was simpler and more beautiful. By reshaping his landscapes with woodlands, meadows, and vast swaths of mowed lawns, he artificially created "natural" landscapes. Large sweeps of monoculture

One goal of climate-friendly gardening is to create native plant "corridors" to support native birds such as the Carolina chickadee as well as butterflies and other native fauna.

lawn grass soon became status symbols for the wealthy. Not long after that, suburban middle-class homeowners followed suit. The lawn continues to this day to be a symbol of pride and, for some, a kind of happy obsession.

There are many reasons to consider reducing the size of our lawns or eliminating them altogether. Because monoculture lawns aren't found in nature, they're not inherently robust. To grow a perfect lawn, a homeowner often has to resort to synthetic fertilizers, pesticides, herbicides, and fungicides. In fact, homeowners apply far more pesticides per acre than farmers do.

These chemicals kill pollinators, especially the ones that build their nests in the ground. They kill insects, which birds depend on for food. Lawn chemicals destroy earthworms, caterpillars, butterflies, ladybugs, lightning bugs, honeybees, spiders, and a host of soil organisms. The poisoned insects and weeds are eaten by other wildlife such as turtles, frogs, birds, and other creatures and end up poisoning them as well.

The runoff from lawns pollutes our waterways. Lawns constantly fertilized and treated with other chemicals are living in an unhealthy soil environment, in which they become dependent on these human inputs in order to survive. And, if those aren't enough reasons to consider the dangers of lawn chemicals, we have our own human health to consider as well. Because they are endocrine disrupters, pesticides have been associated with autism, diabetes, cancer, and ADHD.

Another downside to lawns is that we tend to overirrigate them. According to the U.S. Department of Agriculture, nearly half of American homeowners' water usage goes to lawns. One way to avoid this extravagant use of water is to take advantage of the lawn's built-in strategy for dealing with extreme heat or cold by allowing it to go dormant naturally. Watering, fertilizing, and mowing stimulates growth and runs counter to the idea of dormancy.

If a lawn is something you don't quite want to forsake, there are alternatives to a traditional lawn grass monoculture. Consider creating a healthy, biodiverse community by mingling native grasses with clovers, sedges, straggler daisies, violets, and dandelions. The result will be much better pest and disease resistance, healthier soil, better heat tolerance, and less need for fertilizer. These plants will also provide pollen, nectar, and larval food for native insects. Flowering lawns are more resilient to the environmental pressures of climate change than monoculture lawns.

There are a few native alternatives to traditional lawn grass, which will give a less manicured look but, if kept mowed, will still provide an open expanse of green that can be walked on. Gardeners are experimenting with natives once considered to be weeds, such as common carpet grass (*Axonopus fissifolius*), nimble will (*Muhlenbergia schreberi*), and blanket grass (*Axonopus compressus*). These plants tolerate poor and compacted soils as well as shade, and they stand up well to heat, drought, and flooding. Straggler daisy (*Calyptocarpus vialis*) also grows in poor soil and tolerates shade; small yellow flowers in summer are a bonus. (See appendix for details on recommended native grasses and groundcovers.)

Among the more traditional lawn grasses, the most drought tolerant are Bermuda grass (*Cynodon dactylon*) and Bahia grass (*Paspalum notatum*). In winter, rather than overseeding the lawn with ryegrass, allow it to go dormant.

If you do have a lawn, consider switching from a gas-powered mower to a muscle-powered push mower or an electric mulching mower, which allows the cut grass to decay in place and replenishes the soil. This self-mulching will also cut down on the need for fertilizer. The higher you mow your grass, the deeper roots it will develop and the less watering it will need. A good rule of thumb is to set the mower blades at three inches and remove only one-third of the height at a time. Sharp mower blades will reduce water loss as well—lawn grass is less stressed by a sharp cut than by the tearing that happens with dull blades. (See chapter 8 for details on weaning ourselves off of power tools and chemicals.)

If you choose to irrigate your lawn, the best practice is to do it only when needed and then during the coolest part of the day to avoid water loss through evaporation. (See chapter 9 for details on irrigation and water usage.)

CHAPTER SIX

Choosing What to Plant

By increasing the natural-ness of our landscape we become a positive force in contributing to a sustain-able world.

—Donald Harker,
Landscape Restoration Handbook

THE SOUTHEAST IS one of the most biodiverse regions in the country, with thousands of native plants to choose from. There are also a number of well-adapted nonnatives that have proven successful in our gardens over the decades and, more import-ant, have shown themselves to be noninvasive. Although they don't always provide the same range of benefits to wildlife as na-tives do, they're part of the current reality of many southeastern gardens, and we need to take them into account.

Regardless of what plant palette you're choosing from, the most important planting rule is that the plants be suited to the area in which you plan to grow them. Plants situated in the wrong place are more prone to diseases and pests. The "wrong place" can mean too much or not enough sun, too much or not enough water, overly rich or overly poor soil, temperatures too hot or too cold for a plant's survival, and factors such as drought or flooding, which certain plants can't tolerate. Plants installed in the wrong place will fail to thrive.

Knowing what to plant where means thinking about a number of key factors: What U.S. Department of Agriculture (USDA) zone do you garden in? Are you gardening in the Mountains, the Piedmont, or the Coastal Plain? What's your native soil like? Do you need to factor in the urban heat island effect? Are you living in a flood zone or a hurricane-prone area? And, just as important, what are all the different microclimates of your unique gardening space? Is one part of your garden always cooler/hotter/wetter/dryer/windier than another?

A delicate plant such as nodding trillium (*Trillium cernuum*), for example, is perfectly suited to dappled sunlight and moist well-drained soil in a USDA Zone 7 North Carolina mountainside garden. Its chances of survival would be slim to none in a USDA Zone 9 full-sun, dry, sandy garden of coastal Georgia. Similarly, the bright red-and-yellow beach blanketflower (*Gaillardia pulchella*) thriving in the heat of an Alabama coastal summer would soon give up the ghost in the deep shade and constantly moist soil of, say, a Tennessee mountain stream-bank garden. It's important to understand exactly which plants thrive in your general geographical area and in your garden's particular microclimates. Here are some basic considerations.

USDA Zones

Sixty-odd years ago the USDA divided the country into growing zones, allowing us to anticipate the likely coldest winter temperatures for our geographical area and to plant accordingly. The majority of the southeastern United States falls between USDA Zones 5a and 9b (with the southern part of Florida zoned 9b–11a). There are two problems with this system: (1) knowing your USDA zone won't help you predict the highest summer temperatures,

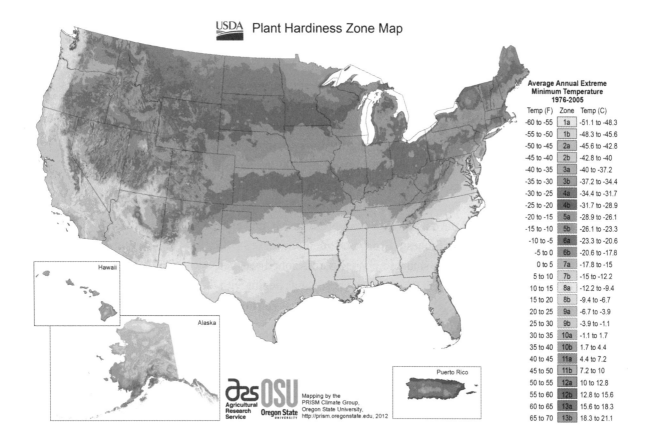

USDA Plant Hardiness Zone Map

Average Annual Extreme Minimum Temperature 1976-2005

Temp (F)	Zone	Temp (C)
-60 to -55	1a	-51.1 to -48.3
-55 to -50	1b	-48.3 to -45.6
-50 to -45	2a	-45.6 to -42.8
-45 to -40	2b	-42.8 to -40
-40 to -35	3a	-40 to -37.2
-35 to -30	3b	-37.2 to -34.4
-30 to -25	4a	-34.4 to -31.7
-25 to -20	4b	-31.7 to -28.9
-20 to -15	5a	-28.9 to -26.1
-15 to -10	5b	-26.1 to -23.3
-10 to -5	6a	-23.3 to -20.6
-5 to 0	6b	-20.6 to -17.8
0 to 5	7a	-17.8 to -15
5 to 10	7b	-15 to -12.2
10 to 15	8a	-12.2 to -9.4
15 to 20	8b	-9.4 to -6.7
20 to 25	9a	-6.7 to -3.9
25 to 30	9b	-3.9 to -1.1
30 to 35	10a	-1.1 to 1.7
35 to 40	10b	1.7 to 4.4
40 to 45	11a	4.4 to 7.2
45 to 50	11b	7.2 to 10
50 to 55	12a	10 to 12.8
55 to 60	12b	12.8 to 15.6
60 to 65	13a	15.6 to 18.3
65 to 70	13b	18.3 to 21.1

Mapping by the PRISM Climate Group, Oregon State University, http://prism.oregonstate.edu, 2012

Most recent USDA plant hardiness zone map

a factor that may have much greater significance in the South than in the North, and (2) U.S. climate zones are steadily shifting northward.

The current USDA zone map, revised in 2012, reveals that almost half the country had warmer average temperatures in 2012 than in 1990, when the previous edition of the map was published. As global warming continues, gardeners will have to make their own calculations, based on observation and experience, about the reality of their climate zones. This matters for decisions such as which plants to choose, when to plant seedlings, when to harvest vegetables, and when to expect frost.

An excellent strategy when choosing plants for your garden is to favor those whose range has as its midpoint the zone in which you garden. For example, if you garden in Zone 7, you'll normally have great success with plants that are zoned USDA 6–8. Another way of looking at this guideline is to choose plants at least one zone colder and one zone hotter. Again, with Zone 7 as an example, you would be safest to *not* choose plants whose USDA zone range begins or ends with seven, because that wouldn't allow for weather extremes. Ensuring that your zone falls in the middle of the plants' USDA zone range grants room for year-to-year volatility.

As the climate warms, it will become increasingly inadvisable to choose plants that have your USDA zone as their southernmost point, because it's likely that your zone will shift. For example, if you live in what's now Zone 8 (which may well morph into Zone 9 as climate change advances), don't assume that plants such as dropwort (Zones 3–8) or wood anemone (Zones 5–8) will thrive. Although it might seem smart to choose plants zoned warmer than your current rating (e.g., trying to grow plants whose range begins with USDA Zone 9 in an area currently zoned 8), experts advise against this because the winter temperatures of Zone 8 are still likely to dip too low for Zone 9 plants to survive.

Natives

For many decades landscapers have relied on a limited, homogeneous palette of nonnative trees and shrubs, because they're so easy to obtain and because they're often touted as being pest free. These old standbys often require supplemental water, fertilization, and regular application of, yes, pesticides, making them climate-unfriendly choices. If they're truly pest free, this means they don't support local insects or the web of animals dependent on those insects. These introduced aliens may not provide larval food, nectar, fruits, berries, seeds, or other critical resources for native insects, pollinators, birds, or other wildlife. And what's worse, they may escape into the wild and overwhelm native ecosystems.

Native plants, on the other hand, are rich in ecological services, meaning that they support native wildlife, contribute to healthy soil biomes, reduce air and soil pollution, mitigate severe climate events, and store carbon. Rick Darke and Doug Tallamy, in their book *The Living Landscape*, define a native

Plant native perennials such as coreopsis in large groupings for better design effect and to make them easier for pollinators to locate.

plant as one that "has evolved in a given place over a period of time sufficient to develop complex and essential relationships with the physical environment and other organisms in a given ecological community."

There are many reasons to fill the garden with plants native to your area. Certain insects, birds, and animals have interdependent relationships with these plants. Certain butterfly and beetle larvae feed on very specific native species and are unable to take advantage of the exotics in the garden.

Natives are disappearing due to development, agribusiness, and other human activities. It's estimated that 15 percent of native plants in the continental United States are presently at risk of extinction. When natives disappear, this decimates the wildlife populations that depend on them. Doug Tallamy and his students have found that planting native trees, shrubs, perennials, and grasses increases the benefits to your backyard wildlife by a factor of almost thirty compared to plantings of nonnative exotics. Every one of us can turn our yards into a piece of this jigsaw puzzle, contributing new native corridors for wildlife.

As Tallamy says in *Bringing Nature Home*, "[There are] simply not enough native plants left in the 'wild'—that is not enough undisturbed habitat remaining in the United States—to support the diversity of wildlife most of us would like to see survive into the distant future."

Another native plant advocate, Benjamin Vogt, argues that a garden that's planted with 100 percent natives can be considered restrictive only if we look at it from the point of view of our own species. In *A New Garden Ethic*, he says, "The native plant discussion forces us to think of our landscapes with a deeper purpose, and especially asks us to consider lives and voices other than our own."

Finding Natives Suitable for Your Area

In addition to using the charts found in this book (see appendix) and in the recommended reading (see chapter 12) or conducting general online research, an excellent source of information on native plants for your growing areas is the National Wildlife Federation's Native Plant Finder (www.nwf .org/nativeplantfinder). It provides a list of native plants by zip code. Or visit the Biota of North America Program website (www.bonap.org) for an extensive county-by-county listing of over 24,000 native plants growing in the wild. Audubon also has a native plants database (https://www.audubon.org /native-plants) that allows you to find plants and sort by zip code.

Many states also offer their own flora dot maps, which indicate where in the state a particular native has been recorded and how extensive that native plant population is.

If you're able to acquire plants that were grown in the South, ideally within your own ecoregion, your state, or two neighboring states, the plants will have experienced similar growing conditions to your own, and you'll have better luck with their survival. In addition, you'll save on transportation and packaging, thus reducing the carbon footprint of acquiring plants. Check with your local native plant society to find good sources and to learn about upcoming plant sales and plant swaps. A good selection of native

Examples of Native Fast-Growing Trees

Chickasaw plum
(*Prunus angustifolia*)

Laurel oak (*Quercus laurifolia*)

Purpleleaf sand cherry
(*Prunus × cistena*)

Redbud (*Cercis canadensis*)

Red mulberry (*Morus rubra*)

River birch (*Betula nigra*)

plants is becoming increasingly available online as well. And next time you visit your local nursery, tell them you're interested in buying native plants.

Trees

Native trees are the stars of the climate-friendly garden. First, they provide shelter and food for wildlife, and because they're long-lived, they can provide ecosystem services over a greater period of time than other plants. Their deep roots prevent erosion. They absorb storm-water runoff and store carbon in their roots, trunks, branches, and leaves. A deciduous tree planted on the south side of the house provides insulation, cooling both the soil and the air in the warm months and allowing sun to warm the house once the leaves drop in the fall. In the Southeast, where severe weather events are predicted

Examples of Native Slow-Growing, Long-Lived Trees

American beech (*Fagus grandifolia*)

American hop hornbeam (*Ostrya virginiana*)

Blackgum (*Nyssa sylvatica*)

Hickory (*Carya* spp.)

Maple (*Acer* spp.)

Oak (*Quercus* spp.)

Yellow birch (*Betula alleghaniensis*)

Yellowwood (*Cladrastis kentukea*)

Live oak, which once dominated many areas of the Southeast, provides abundant ecological services and is a keystone species of its ecosystem.

to become more frequent, trees serve to slow down the rain's impact and prevent flood-caused soil erosion.

Where cities are suffering from the urban heat island effect, trees are a vital part of the solution. They not only absorb harmful particulates in the air and buffer city noises, but their shade limits the formation of ground-level ozone. They also modulate the sharp variations in temperature caused by heat waves.

There are many native trees—as well as shrubs, which can be grown into small trees—that tolerate urban conditions in the Southeast (see appendix for details).

Choosing trees that provide dappled sunlight will allow you to use the area underneath to grow a host of native plants that prefer partial sun. If you have a sizable space that's not already landscaped, you might plant native trees for succession so that the faster-growing species will eventually be succeeded by slower-growing, longer-lived ones.

As with every other kind of planting, grouping trees together ultimately creates healthier soil conditions, better disease and pest resistance, and enhanced wind tolerance. In addition, a group of trees can channel cool air. The U.S. Forest Service's Climate Change Tree Atlas (www.fs.fed.us/nrs /atlas) gives excellent guidance on selecting trees with future climate change conditions in mind.

Shrubs

Native shrubs provide beautiful spring and summer blooms, autumn color, and berries or fruit for wildlife in the fall and winter. The shrub layer provides critical nesting sites and cover for birds, stores carbon, absorbs runoff, and filters pollutants. When selecting a native or other shrub for a particular location, think about whether you expect it to stay put and simply grow wider and taller over time or whether you'd like it to help you with your goal of covering the soil with plants. The latter goal is best achieved with colonizing or clonal shrubs. (See appendix for details on trees and shrubs for special conditions such as drought tolerance, flood tolerance, salt tolerance, and urban conditions as well as for details on evergreens and trees and shrubs providing autumn, spring, and summer color.)

Facing page: Oakleaf hydrangea is a native shrub that spreads by underground rhizomes to form colonies over time.

Perennials

By definition, a perennial is a plant that, given the right conditions, will survive for many years in the same spot. This benefits soil health by allowing complex soil structures and their microorganisms to remain undisturbed. Many southeastern native perennials are deep rooted, which gives them an advantage both during times of drought when they can reach deeper sources of moisture and during flooding and high winds when they might otherwise be uprooted.

There are hundreds of native perennials, with abundant choices for gardeners throughout the Mountains, Piedmont, and Coastal Plain. Some bloom briefly in the spring, many others produce flowers on and off all summer, and a number come into bloom in later summer and fall. (See appendix for details of recommended native perennials for various conditions including drought, flood, and salt tolerance as well as autumn bloom color.)

Stokes' aster is among the hundreds of outstanding native perennials that thrive in southeastern gardens.

Grasses

Native sun-loving ornamental grasses, such as bushy bluestem (*Andropogon glomeratus*), pink or purple muhly grass (*Muhlenbergia* spp.), purple love grass (*Eragrostis spectabilis*), northern sea oats (*Chasmanthium latifolium*), and switch grass, among others, develop deep roots, which help them withstand drought and flooding. Often they'll grow on poor soil and are good bets for naturalizing. Some of these same grasses spread by rhizomes or stolons, allowing you to fill in an area fairly rapidly.

In winter the ornamental grasses go dormant, but allowing the dried seed heads to remain on the plants provides food for songbirds and other wildlife. It's best to wait for warmer spring weather if you need to divide or move a native grass. (See appendix for details of recommended native grasses for particular conditions including salt, flood, and drought tolerance.)

Native ornamental grasses such as northern sea oats add drama and texture to the garden. This grass tolerates drought and flood conditions, provides food for birds and small mammals, and is a larval host plant for butterflies.

Ferns

Ferns are a wonderful solution to deep or partial shade. Many of them are colonizers, so they'll fill in as a groundcover even in difficult areas. In fact, if you're having trouble growing a lawn in a shady spot, consider planting ferns instead. Ferns can thrive at the base of trees such as oak, walnut, hickory, and pine, where the tree roots are well spread out. They're great to intermingle with spring ephemeral wild flowers and with native sedges.

Cinnamon fern and royal fern (*Osmunda regalis*) are two spectacular large ferns native to the Southeast, and there are many other equally beautiful species. Among the more delicate native ferns are the maidenhairs (*Adiantum* spp.), woolly fern (*Hemionitis lanosa*), and sensitive fern (*Onoclea sensibilis*). In moist soils some of our native ferns will spread aggressively, which may be just what you want in order to cover as much bare ground as possible. Many will also tolerate dry soil and may be adapted to sunny spots. (See appendix for details.)

Southern shield fern is a drought-tolerant fern that will quickly fill in a shady spot in the garden.

Nativars

For many decades now, plant breeders have been taking native plants, known as "straight species"—that is, plants as they occur in nature, unfiddled with by humans—and altering them in various ways to create bigger, longer-lasting blooms, shorter stature, better heat tolerance, or a new leaf color. These altered natives, or "nativars" as they're sometimes called, are then propagated asexually and sold under trade names. This trend is bringing many more native-based plants into the marketplace and into the home landscape. The question of how these nativars impact pollinators, leaf eaters, and nectar-seeking insects and birds is still being studied. The answer so far is that it varies depending on the particular cultivar. Leaf-eating insects in particular seem to feed on nativars except those whose leaf color has been modified.

Cloned nativars are produced vegetatively with cuttings made from stems, roots, or bulbs of an existing plant, which means they won't provide the kind of genetic variation that occurs with straight species. Some nativars may be sterile. We know that biodiversity in the garden strengthens its overall resistance to diseases, pests, and other stressors, so this is considered one of the drawbacks to nativars. Some other types of nativars are propagated from naturally occurring variants of the straight species and are not sterile. For now, the safest bet is to choose the straight species or a nativar as close as possible in terms of bloom time, leaf color, and plant shape.

Researchers are asking home gardeners to help collect data on how many and which pollinators, birds, and other wildlife are benefiting from the nativars in their gardens. Visit the Chicago Botanic Garden's Budburst website (ww.budburst.org) for more information on how to participate in this and other citizen-scientist garden reporting that helps address climate change issues.

Below: *Baptisia australis* 'Blue Pearls' is a cultivar of the native species—also known as a "nativar."

Adaptability

Choosing native plants adapted to your particular soil and growing zone is an excellent first step. Another powerful strategy for dealing with climate change is to choose plants that are adaptable to changing and extreme conditions: drought, flooding, different soil types, and stressors such as extreme heat and urban pollution. These plants are sometimes called "generalists" because they can handle so many different situations. This is true for natives as well as nonnatives. The Sand Hills and prairies are home to many generalist plants that can withstand the wild fluctuations in temperature, floods, and droughts common to those areas.

Some native plants, just like their nonnative counterparts, are not generalists. They need very specific niche conditions—a certain pH range or soil texture or a particular level of moisture or coolness—and they won't necessarily stand up to climate extremes. When choosing a generalist plant, bear in mind that recommendations concerning USDA zones and regions (Mountains, Piedmont, or Coastal Plain) are still very important for the plant's success. (See appendix for details of generalist native plants.)

Generalist plants such as the black-eyed Susan can tolerate a wide range of growing conditions including full sun, part shade, boggy sites, dry soil, heat, and humidity.

Purple muhly grass is one of dozens of native plants that can tolerate salt spray.

Salt Tolerance

Another consideration for gardeners in the Southeast, especially those who live near the coast, is whether or not a plant is salt tolerant. Hurricane-force winds can carry salt many miles inland. In addition, drainage ditches and sea level rise both can contribute to the salinization of freshwater ecosystems and inland habitats, which can in turn affect plant survivability. (See appendix for details.)

Plant Communities

Even if your goal isn't to restore a natural meadow or prairie, *Landscape Restoration Handbook* by Donald Harker et al. is an excellent source of information on natural plant communities (see chapter 12). Planting in communities, or assemblages of plants that have naturally evolved together, has been shown to produce healthier, more vigorous plants.

Below: Group plants together with their naturally occurring partners. Here, Carolina phlox and purple coneflowers work together to support a healthy ecosystem.

CHOOSING WHAT TO PLANT

Well-Adapted Nonnatives

Climate-friendly gardening begins with planting natives whenever possible. On the other hand, there are nonnative ("exotic") plants that have been thriving in southeastern gardens for centuries because they're naturally suited to the soils, the temperatures, and the general climate found in this part of the country. These well-adapted nonnatives have proven themselves to be noninvasive, which is a key factor in deciding which plants to invite into your garden.

Although these and other exotic, noninvasive standbys are certainly easier for landscapers and homeowners to get hold of, and their growth habits and needs are well known, this is only because they happened to win an earlier popularity contest. Many native shrubs and trees would work just as well. What needs to happen now is for the natives to become more widely available and better recognized by landscapers and home gardeners alike, so that in the near future they'll be the new go-to favorites, eventually phasing

Popular Nonnative Trees and Shrubs Not Found to Be Invasive

Azalea (*Rhododenron* spp.)

Camellia (*Camellia* spp.)

Crape myrtle (*Lagerstroemia indica*)

Hydrangea (*Hydrangea* spp.)

Indian hawthorn (*Raphiolepsis indica*)

Japanese maple (*Acer palmatum*)

Korean boxwood (*Buxus microphylla*)

Kwanzan cherry (*Prunus serrulata* 'Kanzan')

Loropetalum (*Loropetalum chinense*)

Pittosporum (*Pittosporum* spp.)

Rose (*Rosa* spp.)

Star magnolia (*Magnolia stellata*)

Tulip magnolia (*Magnolia × soulangeana*)

Yoshino cherry (*Prunus × yedoensis*)

Indica azaleas are well-adapted, noninvasive southern garden classics.

out some of the exotics. (See appendix for suggested native substitutes for popular nonnative plants.)

Unfortunately, many other "classic" nonnative plants for southern gardens are not as harmless. For many of us, this is a sobering message. We had no idea what we were planting when we brought these into our gardens, and they often came highly recommended by garden experts who touted their unique beauty or ease of culture. Now that we know better, we need to stop bringing them into our gardens.

Plants Listed as Invasive in at Least One State of the Southeast

(Southern Florida classifies many additional species as invasive.)

Autumn olive (Elaeagnus umbellata)

Bradford pear (Pyrus calleryana)

Buckthorn (Rhamnus cathartica)

Butterfly bush (nonsterile species) (Buddleia davidii)

Chinaberry (Melia azedarach)

Chinese holly (Ilex cornuta)

Chinese privet (Ligustrum sinense)

Chinese silver grass (Miscanthus sinensis)

Chinese wisteria (Wisteria sinensis)

Empress tree (Paulownia tomentosa)

English ivy (Hedera helix)

Garlic mustard (Alliaria petiolata)

Golden bamboo (Phyllostachys aurea)

Japanese barberry (Berberis thunbergii)

Japanese blood grass (Imperata cylindrica)

Japanese climbing fern (Lygodium japonicum)

Japanese honeysuckle (Lonicera japonica)

Japanese knotweed (Fallopia japonica)

Japanese privet (Ligustrum japonicum)

Japanese stiltgrass (Microstegium vimineum)

Japanese wisteria (Wisteria floribunda)

Kudzu (Pueraria montana var. lobata)

Lantana (Lantana camara) (esp. Gulf coast states)

Liriope (Liriope muscari)

Mimosa (Albizia julibrissin)

Monkey grass (Liriope spicata)

Multiflora rose (Rosa multiflora)

Nandina (Nandina domestica)

Oleander (Nerium oleander) (esp. Gulf coast states)

Oriental bittersweet (Celastrus orbiculatus)

Pagoda tree (Styphnolobium japonicum)

Periwinkle (Vinca major and V. minor)

Popcorn tree (Triadica sebifera)

Purple loosestrife (Lythrum salicaria)

Russian olive (Elaeagnus angustifolia)

Sweet autumn clematis (Clematis terniflora)

Thorny elaeagnus (Elaeagnus pungens)

Tree of heaven (Ailanthus altissima)

Invasives—Why Should We Care?

We all know that invasive plants are able to take advantage of ecosystems that have been compromised by human development or global warming and that they can quickly outrun the natives. But it's so easy to go about our own gardening business and not worry about that particular problem. If kudzu or Japanese honeysuckle hasn't invaded our own garden, it may seem like someone else's problem. If we see a Bradford pear in bloom at the nursery and it seems like an easy fix for a sunny spot, we may never realize the consequences of its nasty tendency to escape into and take over wild areas.

Invasive plants spread by seeds carried hundreds of miles by the wind or by birds who eat and excrete them. Kew Royal Botanic Gardens, in England, recently reported that the rate of plant and animal extinction on earth is now hundreds of times the normal baseline rate and that 20 percent or more of the world's plants are at risk for extinction through habitat loss, disease, or competition from invasives. The problem is that native woodlands, pine savannas, wetlands, meadows, and other ecosystems are home to plant communities that evolved together in a delicate balance over very long periods of time. Often they can't stand up to the onslaught of an invasive exotic.

Once we learn what the invasive plants are, we should remove them from our own landscapes and from nearby community properties such as parks, schools, churches, and municipal lots whenever we are able. In addition, we should educate our fellow gardeners when we get the chance; unfortunately many of these invasives are still sold in local garden centers.

When a natural area loses trees, shrubs, and other plants to the more aggressive invasives, that ecosystem becomes poorer and is unable to provide wildlife with the food, habitat, cover, and other services it once did. Bands of paid and unpaid laborers spend untold hours trying to eradicate the invasives, a daunting job that often involves the use of herbicides and creates its own large carbon footprint. Even if we don't personally witness acres of strangulation, the invasive problem affects all of us.

A key principle of climate-friendly gardening is to stop planting invasives and to remove them from our gardens. Invasives such as this monster kudzu vine outcompete natives and can destroy entire ecosystems.

Annuals

Climate-friendly gardening puts a premium on a healthy soil ecosystem, which in turn is strengthened by longer-lived groundcovers, perennials, grasses, ferns, shrubs, and trees. Disturbing the soil to install seasonal plantings and adding the fertilizer often needed to keep them in bloom all summer runs counter to this goal. Instead, consider favoring longer-lasting plants over annuals, planting annuals in containers, or planting annuals from seed to avoid disturbing the soil. For annuals grown in the garden bed, use organic fertilizers such as fish emulsion, kelp meal, worm castings, or compost tea in lieu of synthetic fertilizers.

Choose annuals that benefit pollinators. Some good examples include zinnia (*Zinnia elegans*), cosmos (*Cosmos bipinnatus*), annual sunflower (*Helianthus annuus*), cornflower (*Centaurea cyanus*), calendula (*Calendula officinalis*), annual salvia (*Salvia* spp.), snapdragon (*Antirrhinum majus*), marigold (*Tagetes patula*), and nasturtium (*Tropaeolum majus*).

CHAPTER SEVEN

The Importance of Living Soil

It takes hundreds of years for nature to create fertile soil.

—Sue Reed and
    Ginny Stibolt,
    *Climate-Wise
    Landscaping*

WHEN MOST OF US look down at a patch of bare dirt, our imagination tends to stop somewhere at the top two centimeters, where we may notice whether it's brown or red; crumbly, dusty, or hard packed; and dry or moist. On most days, we're not conjuring up the millions of organisms going about their business in a teaspoon-sized area of dirt, and we're not multiplying those organisms out to a mind-boggling number to encompass, say, our whole backyard. Nor are we imagining the honeycomb of pore space down there or the nonstop commerce of mycorrhizae trading their services with plant roots.

Wonderful fungi and bacteria, possibly too numerous for us to hold in our mind for any sustained period of time, are busy getting what they need in the way of carbons and sugars from plant roots and, in exchange, paying back decomposed organic matter the plants can use to get the food *they* need. Fungi and bacteria also aerate the soil; create an optimum structure for plant roots, water, and air to move in; and act as water filters. It's unimaginably busy down there. The soil isn't some sort of afterthought once we've picked out the perfect pink azalea bush. It's actually running the whole show.

Creating and maintaining healthy soil should be one of our main goals in climate-friendly gardening. Living soil sequesters enormous amounts of carbon. It takes hundreds of years for the soil to develop into a fertile, living ecosystem. Ideally it's not compacted but rather contains about 40 percent pore space, where oxygen and water are stored for plants' use. It acts like a sponge, helping plants better withstand both drought and flood conditions.

Although we think of plants as putting their energy into trunks, stems, leaves, and flowers, the truth is that those account for only 20 percent of plants' energy use. The rest goes into developing strong root systems—for absorbing water and food and for withstanding temperature extremes, droughts, and winds. To develop strong roots, the plants need healthy, living soil.

Unamended Soil

In traditional horticulture we've been in the habit of digging up existing soil and incorporating amendments such as manure and compost, under the theory that the richer the soil, the better. If we're planting trees and shrubs native to our own ecoregion, however, the current understanding is that we don't need to add anything into the planting hole other than the original native soil. This is true regardless of whether the soil is sandy, loamy, rocky, mostly clay, or even spongey, wet, and low in nutrients—as long as the plants we've chosen are at home in that type of soil.

Because the soil (regardless of its particular texture or drainage speed) is an intricately developed ecosystem of fungi, bacteria, plant roots, beneficial insects, and microbes when it's healthy and functioning, this isn't

Find out what kind of soil you have and plant what grows naturally in it. This eastern prickly-pear cactus grows happily in sandy locations including beach dunes.

something we want to disturb if we can help it. Rototilling and double digging tear apart the soil's structure, disturbing the roots that were holding it together. When soil is severely damaged by overtilling, we end up with erosion and water runoff.

Researchers have found an added benefit to low-till or no-till soils, namely that temperatures in the surface soil layers are cooler than those in tilled soil. This is of huge benefit during heat waves and droughts.

Although unamended soil works in many situations, there are exceptions. For example, if tests reveal that you have toxic soil containing heavy metals or other unusual harmful chemicals, you'll need to remove the toxic soil or consider using raised beds. You'll also want to amend your soil with organic matter if all of the healthy topsoil has been removed during the construction of your home and you're left with inorganic subsoil or bedrock. Other places that soil would need organic amendment are where there has been serious soil compaction, excavation, erosion, or depletion/exhaustion through overuse or where there is elevated salt content. The concept of planting in unamended soil is based on the assumption that you are working with healthy native soil.

The key is to find plants suited to the kind of soil you have. Clearly not all plants will do well, or even survive, in the "wrong" native soil. For example, a boggy native soil would support autumn sneezeweed (*Helenium autumnale*) or buttonbush (*Cephalanthus occidentalis*) but would be inhospitable to beach rosemary (*Conradina canescens*) or the palmlike coontie plant (*Zamia integrifolia*), which need well-drained soil. Dry, shallow, rocky soil, on the other hand, would support native butterfly weed or scarlet bee balm (*Monarda didyma*) but make life very challenging for cardinal flower (*Lobelia cardinalis*). So it's a question of matching the right plants to whatever native soil you're working with.

In prior decades, gardeners were strongly advised to amend the native soil with organic matter such as compost, manure, greensand, and other amendments every time they planted anything in the garden. Better yet, they were advised to dig up the entire garden bed and amend it before planting. The better thinking is to find out what type of soil you already have and—assuming it's healthy, living soil—pair it with plants that grow naturally in those conditions. Tests have shown that plants in native soil exhibit better root development and stronger growth on a consistent basis.

Because this idea runs contrary to what garden experts have been advocating for years, it deserves some further explanation. When we dig a hole, say for a tree, and backfill it with a mix of compost, manure, topsoil purchased from the garden center, shredded bark, or any other soil amendment, we create an artificially rich environment for the tree roots. Although the tree initially loves this coddling, this enrichment comes with a number of disadvantages:

1. As the roots grow and they reach the borderline between the amended soil and the native soil, they'll be prone to stay in the more nutrient-rich, better-aerated hole rather than expanding outward into the surrounding soil. This may result in the roots circling around and around inside the amended hole, eventually hardening into that shape. This prevents roots from expanding outward and downward—something they need to do in order to create stability, access water, and continue their growth. These congested roots mean a weak, unstable, unhealthy tree or shrub, which will eventually perish.

2. The difference in water absorption/retention capabilities between the soil in the amended hole and the surrounding native soil may be such that one of two things happens. Either the amended hole has a higher water absorption rate and turns into a water container, staying wet and drowning the plant roots, or if it has less absorption ability than the surrounding soil, water is wicked away, leaving the amended hole dry. This can damage or kill the plant through dehydration.

3. Once the organic matter in the amended planting hole decomposes over time, the ground naturally sinks down and can create a crater effect, which allows water to pool. This sitting water, recurring frequently enough, can cause damage and eventual plant death.

Although these negative effects of soil amendment are easiest to see and understand with trees, the same principles apply to shrubs, perennials, and other garden plants. Assuming you've chosen plants that thrive in your native soil, your plants will have longer lives, more disease resistance, and better drought tolerance—and they'll be more likely to increase in number and size—without soil amendments. (Note that vegetables need amended soil; see chapter 10.)

Vegetables need well-amended organic soil in order to produce well.

Types of Native Soil

With all of the above considerations in mind, our goal becomes first to understand what kind of soil we have and then to learn which native plants naturally evolved to grow in that soil. A couple of quick and easy tricks can help you get started. First, grab a handful of your soil and squeeze it. If it retains its shape like a ball, it's clay. If it trickles through your fingers, it's sand. If it bunches up firmly but is still loose, it's loam. Your soil may well be somewhere on the spectrum of these three. Different parts of your gardening space may have different soil textures.

To find out how fast your soil drains, (1) dig a hole one foot wide by one foot deep with straight sides; (2) fill the hole with water and let it drain completely; (3) fill the hole with water again and measure exactly how deep the water is; and (4) time how long it takes for the water to drain completely. If it drains out at one to three inches per hour, you have "well-drained soil." If it's slower than this, you've got soil that tends to stay wet and will support only plants that don't need well-drained soil. If your soil drains faster than this, it may be on the dry side and may not support plants that need "moist, well-drained soil."

The plant charts in the appendix of this book indicate which native plants need moist well-drained soil, which can tolerate occasional periods of wet soil and flooding, and which prefer dry soil and can tolerate some drought. Your soil may be naturally rich in organic matter or relatively poor. The pH may tend more toward acidic or basic. Some native plants have a wide tolerance within these ranges, and some have more specific needs. Finding plants that thrive in whatever type of soil you have is an excellent first step in climate-friendly gardening.

How to Plant in Native Soil

When planting small seeds it's only necessary to rake the soil surface, cover with a thin layer of soil, and water well. Larger seeds can be planted in furrows, but it's not necessary to dig up an entire area to plant seeds.

When planting seedlings, bulbs, perennials, ornamental grasses, ferns, shrubs, or trees, only dig up as much soil as necessary for the roots to fit

Spotted bee balm is one of hundreds of natives that perform beautifully in unamended soil.

with a little extra space. Contrary to earlier gardening wisdom, there's no need to dig a hole three times the size of the root mass.

Don't add fertilizer or soil amendments to the planting hole. Make sure the flare (the area where the roots and crown meet) is level with the surrounding soil, then backfill with the soil you just removed. It's important to water deeply at planting time to ensure there are no air pockets.

Root Washing

In the case of containerized trees and shrubs, there's a fairly new planting practice gaining popularity: root washing. (This process is not recommended, however, for field-grown balled and burlapped trees.) Root washing of containerized trees and shrubs involves soaking the plant in water in a bucket overnight and then rinsing off most or all of the growing medium with a gentle spray of water to expose the plant's root structure.

The first reason to do this is to see if the roots are circling the container, making it "pot bound," which is generally a slow death sentence for plants. If the roots are pot bound, prune them carefully to allow them to expand outward and downward as they grow.

Second, by seeing where the roots meet the crown at the flare, it's easier to install the flare level with the ground and not buried beneath the surface, which would also mean eventual death.

Another advantage of root washing is that the roots will move into the native soil without the temptation of confining themselves to the extra-rich growing medium. The newly planted trees or shrubs will also put energy into root establishment rather than into stems, leaves, and flowers—a great benefit to the plant in the long run as it meets environmental stressors.

Once the plant is in the hole with the flare at ground level, backfill with the native soil you removed, tamp down lightly, and water thoroughly. One way of ensuring that the planting hole doesn't sink down after planting is to add soil and water in stages. As mentioned above, give the tree or shrub a thorough soaking at the time of planting to eliminate air pockets.

Because some roots may be damaged in the process of root washing, it's important to pay attention to watering the plant during the first year.

Compost and Mulch

Even though digging extra-large holes and adding amendments at planting time is not recommended, gardeners can still help the existing soil organisms and allow for continued soil health by adding compost as a top dressing. Placing a ring of compost around the drip line of trees and shrubs or in between and around smaller plants will provide a natural, slow-release soil amendment over time similar to what plants would receive from decaying matter in a more natural setting.

Adding a layer of organic mulch will help conserve water, mitigate against temperature extremes, and eventually add organic matter to the soil as the mulch decomposes.

COMPOST

Compost is available commercially, or you can create your own with leftover food scraps and yard waste. The general formula is a mixture of two to three parts carbon-rich "brown" materials (dead leaves, straw, twigs, chopped woody stems, paper, sawdust) to one part nitrogen-rich "green" materials (grass clippings, green leaves, kitchen scraps [but not meat], coffee grounds, eggshells, aged cow or poultry manure). Keep the compost moist but not wet, and add in some soil from your garden to provide bacteria and microbes necessary for digestion of the material.

Keep the compost aerated by turning it regularly. It's ready to use when it's dark brown, crumbly, and pleasant smelling. Compost that reaches an internal temperature of 140 degrees ensures that most weed seeds and pathogens have been killed.

Below: Leaf mold, which mimics natural decaying matter on the forest floor, is a perfect mulch.

MULCH

Organic mulches around trees, shrubs, and other plants keep the ground cooler and help retain moisture. They discourage weeds and benefit the soil organisms as they decompose. If you're putting down a layer of compost, you can put the mulch layer on top of that. There are many excellent organic mulches to choose from.

LEAF MOLD

Leaf mold is the term used for leaves that have been decomposing for six months to a year. Shredding the leaves first and keeping the leaf pile watered will speed up the process. Leaf mold is one of the best possible additions you can use in a climate-friendly garden. It's free and available without fossil fuel transportation costs. It has a powerful ability to increase the soil's water retention, it fosters beneficial soil organisms, and it improves soil structure. It's an outstanding compost—making good use of all the fallen leaves and enriching the soil in a very natural way.

PINE STRAW

Pine straw (fallen pine needles) is an excellent mulch and is readily available in most parts of the Southeast. Because no trees are cut down, pine straw removal is sustainable. It's most often used as a mulch under trees and shrubs but can also be used as a mulch in garden beds. (Note: The old thinking that pine straw would acidify the soil underneath it has been disproved. There's no need to limit its use to azaleas, camellias, and other acid-loving plants.)

PINE BARK MULCH

Pine bark mulch comes in many forms and textures. The most finely shredded, which is sold as "soil conditioner," works well for garden and vegetable beds. The largest size (pine bark nuggets) covers a larger area more quickly and lasts slightly longer than the finely shredded pine bark, but it poses a problem in flood-prone areas because of its tendency to float away. Artificially colored mulches are often made from recycled wood and may be contaminated with toxic chemicals.

Instead of covering bare areas with mulch, consider planting native groundcovers, which sequester carbon, stabilize the soil, and benefit wildlife. Seen here is the groundcover green-and-gold.

AVOID SYNTHETIC WEED BARRIER
CLOTHS AND LANDSCAPE FABRIC

Landscape fabric is a poor idea for many reasons. It's made from fossil fuel materials, so it has a large carbon footprint. It's been found to reduce the flow of CO_2 and oxygen between soil and atmosphere, which makes it detrimental to soil health. The organic mulch that normally sits on top of landscape fabric (to hide it) tends to blow off or be washed out of place in downpours. Weeds and strong woody plants find a way to grow through landscape fabric and become entangled when you try to remove them. What's more, landscaping fabric laid down at the time of tree planting can girdle the trunk and roots as the tree grows.

CYPRESS MULCH IS NOT AN
EARTH-FRIENDLY ALTERNATIVE

Cypress swamps are being harvested to meet the increasing demand for cypress mulch, which means damage to and weakening of an important natural ecosystem. Not only does this process destroy plant and animal habitats, but it also weakens a very important defense against hurricane storm surge. In the Gulf coast region, where much of the cypress mulch is harvested, cypress swamps are essential players in absorbing storm surge flooding and wind force. There's no reason to use cypress mulch when there are so many other excellent alternatives.

SHREDDED RUBBER MULCH

Shredded rubber mulch, made from recycled tires, has its pros and cons. Its major advantage is that it recycles material that might otherwise end up in a landfill. As a mulch it helps to retain moisture, keeps the soil cooler, and suppresses weeds. It's now being used extensively on playgrounds for its durability and elasticity. The drawbacks for gardens include the fact that it doesn't add organic matter to the soil through decomposition and it leaches heavy metals, minerals, and toxic chemicals used in the tire manufacturing process. These leachates are taken up by plant roots and can migrate to nearby bodies of water, harming aquatic life.

PEBBLES AND ROCKS

Pebbles and rocks used as a mulch have the advantage of being permanent, but they do nothing to improve the soil or add organic matter to the garden. They tend to retain heat longer than other mulches, and from a practical point of view when weeds grow up in between, as they most surely will, the gardener may well be tempted to turn to harmful chemicals to keep the pebbles neat looking.

NEWSPAPER AND CARDBOARD

Laying down corrugated cardboard is often used as a way to kill all vegetation in a large area before planting, but the drawback is that this process isn't good for the soil. Much of the corrugated cardboard in which our packages are shipped is coated for durability. This coating creates an impermeable barrier that doesn't allow gases to pass between the soil and the atmosphere and repels water. For a period of three months or so until the cardboard breaks down completely, this material is depriving soil organisms of the conditions they need to survive. This results in unhealthy, unbalanced soil.

Although putting down several layers of newspaper works when creating lasagna soil for a vegetable garden (see chapter 10)—because the newspaper will be covered with organic material and kept moist—it isn't recommended for use as a "mulch" in other parts of the garden.

Peat Moss Is Not a Climate-Friendly Soil Amendment

Peatlands (made up of peat bogs and fens) are a subset of wetlands that act as massive carbon sinks for the planet, storing a third of the world's soil carbon and thereby lessening the effects of global warming. They also prevent flooding, act as water purifiers, provide nesting and migratory flyways for birds, and serve as spawning grounds for some fish species and habitats for other fauna. The peat layers take hundreds or thousands of years to develop, growing only one-sixteenth of an inch per year.

Harvesting peat releases large amounts of CO_2 into the atmosphere, and some of the mined land continues to release CO_2 afterward. The process involves draining the wetlands and stripping off the top living layer of sphagnum moss, which is a habitat for a complex web of flora and fauna, in order to get to the decayed moss underneath.

Canadian peat producers (from whom the United States gets approximately 80 percent of its supply) argue that they're regenerating the peatlands after harvesting the peat and that their practice is therefore sustainable. However, ecologists believe that the damage caused by draining the wetlands and destroying the habitat of unique plants and animals cannot be undone.

From a practical gardening standpoint, we don't need to use peat. Compost, aged manure, and leaf mold are excellent substitutes. Peat doesn't provide plants with any nutrients. An added disadvantage is that when it dries out it can be very hard to rewet.

Note: Instead of using peat pots for starting seedlings, try coconut coir. It has similar water retention properties and, being nonacidic, it is actually more supportive of seedlings.

CHAPTER EIGHT

Weaning Ourselves off Toxic Chemicals and Gas-Powered Tools

We have spent the last half century proving beyond the shadow of a doubt that a sterile garden does not work.

—Doug Tallamy,
Bringing Nature Home

THE HOME GARDEN INDUSTRY makes a tidy profit selling us chemicals for our gardens. Many of us have tool sheds lined with herbicides for keeping our driveways and sidewalks neat, pesticides for killing aphids, slugs, mites, and scales, and fungicides for treating leaf spot and powdery mildew. Our attraction to these products is understandable. We've been raised on the notion that our gardens should be perfect, that chewed leaf margins or dandelions in the lawn or spotty hydrangea leaves are ruining our dream. In order to wean ourselves off of these chemicals we really need to adjust our idea of what a beautiful garden should be.

A garden is a refuge, an oasis of beauty and calm, a place to restore the soul and the psyche. We get joy from making our gardens aesthetically pleasing. For some people this is a more orderly, controlled look; for others it's more exuberant and flowing. All of these things can be achieved with the added bonus of mitigating climate change, enriching the ecosystem we garden in, and bringing ourselves into a deeper relationship with nature.

For many of us, this means reimagining our dream gardens as places where it's OK for leaves to be chewed by insects, where funky dried brown flower heads are allowed to hang out all winter, and where mysterious impenetrable thickets coexist with our more orderly flower beds. Reimagining our ideal garden may also involve finding and using plants we hadn't previously known about, figuring out how to do without some of our past practices, and reconnecting with our fellow creatures on a more intimate level.

Weeds

Many weeds (e.g., quack grass, Johnson grass, lamb's-quarters, Canada thistle, plantain, and jimsonweed) respond to the increase in CO_2 in the atmosphere by growing faster and more prolifically. Warmer weather also spurs weed growth, and weeds will be migrating northward just like other, more desirable plants. As climate-friendly gardeners, we can deal with this threat without resorting to toxic chemicals.

A weed is basically a plant growing where we don't want it to grow. But in the soil where that weed grows are billions of living organisms that will be harmed or killed by synthetic herbicides such as glyphosate (sold as Roundup, Brush Killer, GroundClear, and others). The dead soil is, in turn, less able to absorb water and leads to increased runoff and pollution of waterways. In addition, the death of soil organisms releases carbon into the air. Another hazard of using weed killers is the collateral damage to clovers and other pollinator-friendly plants in the lawn and damage to nearby desirable trees, shrubs, and perennials.

Scientists continue to debate the extent to which synthetic herbicides pose a danger to the health of humans and pets. Alternative, nontoxic weed killers for small spots include boiling water or a mixture of salt, vinegar, and dish soap. But even these home remedies can be toxic to fauna such as toads and worms.

Instead of using herbicides in the garden and on our lawns, there are other things to try. The first and best idea would be to cover the ground with plants of your own choosing. There are many fast-spreading natives, low, medium, and tall in height, that will happily oblige. In lawns, the climate-friendly choice is to allow dandelions, clovers, violets, and other plants to coexist with the turfgrass. They are a food resource for pollinators and other insects, and they can be kept in check by periodic mowing.

As you wait for your chosen groundcovers and taller plants to grow in, the best practice is to remove weeds by hand. If you cut them off at the base rather than pulling them, you get the added bonus of not exposing or encouraging the next layer of dormant weed seeds. Where there's bare earth, topping it off with a layer of mulch will act as a weed suppressant until you can fill it in with a native groundcover or other planting. But as suggested earlier, we want to leave some nonmulched bare soil in back corners for the native bees and wasps that nest in it.

Although using landscaping fabric or weed cloth seems like it would be a good alternative to synthetic weed killers, it isn't recommended for the reasons explained earlier in the section on compost and mulch.

Beneficial Insects versus Pests

Doug Tallamy reminds us in *Bringing Nature Home* that it "may be hard to admit, but we need healthy insect populations to ensure our own survival." In traditional gardening, flying and crawling insects, caterpillars, bugs, and beetles have been either ignored, lumped into the general category of pests, or occasionally revered—as in the case of the now iconic yellow-white-and-black-striped caterpillar, which morphs into an orange-and-black monarch butterfly. Pollinators such as bees, ants, moths, flies, and beetles are often overlooked or inadvertently destroyed in the attempt to rid the garden of pests. As with so many other aspects of gardening life, this is an area in which we can shift our thinking. If we're looking at the garden as an interdependent web of life, then every ant gets to play a role.

Chemical eradication of pests can indiscriminately harm beneficial insects and pollinators. Here an adult female eastern black swallowtail visits a native purple coneflower.

As we saw earlier, between 75 percent and 95 percent of flowering plants depend on animal pollination, as does one-third of the world's food supply. If we're lovers of flowers, flowering shrubs and trees, fruits, and nuts of all sorts, we're reliant on insects and other fauna for their service to us as pollinators. Indiscriminate spraying, including spraying yards for mosquito suppression, is devastating to pollinators and other beneficial insects.

Pests

Many insects are moving to new habitats farther north or at higher altitudes, although not all are capable of this kind of adaptation. Some insect pests and disease organisms that normally make an annual south–north round trip are now able to do so earlier in the year and reach farther. Longer periods of warm weather also favor increased numbers of insect generations, and warm winters may allow some cold-sensitive insect pests to overwinter. The further bad news is that extreme events such as heat waves and drought will favor outbreaks of certain pests and pest-borne pathogens. Either because of changes in temperature or changes in natural range, predators that normally control certain insect pests may be absent or less efficient in doing their job.

INTEGRATED PEST MANAGEMENT

Integrated pest management is a process developed for farmers and widely used now by home gardeners, which recognizes that not all insects need to be "controlled." There are three basic steps:

1. Prevent harmful pests by choosing well-adapted plants, including natives, and placing them in suitable conditions by encouraging beneficial insects and removing diseased plant material.

2. Monitor for pests, understanding that control is not the same as eradication. See how much damage has been done and educate yourself on what will happen if the plant is left untreated.

3. Use the least toxic pest control method.

ORGANIC PEST CONTROLS

Without resorting to toxic chemicals, there are a number of ways to control pests that are attacking your plants. First, handpick any bugs you see or hit the plant with a strong spray of water from the hose. Use floating row covers to deter larger pests such as squash bugs and beetles. Place cardboard collars in the ground around vulnerable plants to discourage cutworms and slugs.

Plant herbs such as angelica, dill, tansy, and coriander, as well as native yarrow and annual sunflowers, to attract beneficial insects, which will feast on aphids and other pests. Lacewings, ladybugs, spiders, wasps, and various ground beetles all play a role in keeping harmful pests under control. Add onions and garlic to your garden to deter weevils, spider mites, and other harmful insects. Try planting radishes to deter cucumber beetles, borage to deter tomato hornworms and cabbage moths, and hyacinth beans to repel leaf-footed bugs.

Although commercial **insecticidal soaps** are effective against certain pests on contact, they can also cause photosensitivity in leaves, especially in hot weather, and they can be harmful to bee populations. Spraying plants with a homemade mixture of dish soap and water isn't recommended, because it may damage plants by dissolving the waxy cuticle of the leaves.

Popular, plant-based **pyrethrin** insecticides have the unfortunate side effect of killing beneficial insects and are not recommended. Plant-based **neem-oil** products are effective against certain insect pests, provided the spray makes direct contact, but they can be harmful to bees.

Microbe-based **Bt** (*Bacillus thuringiensis*) is effective when applied at the larval stage of insect development and doesn't harm beneficial insects or present risks of toxicity to other animals. **Horticultural oil** sprayed on plants will smother certain sucking insects such as aphids and scales and is not harmful to bees or other beneficial insects. To be on the safe side, apply organic pesticides and fungicides on a nonwindy day, when rain is not imminent, and when temperatures range between fifty and eighty degrees.

Avoid using **sticky traps** (boards, tubes, or tape covered in sticky glue). They not only capture insect pests but trap small birds, bats, lizards, snakes, and beneficial insects, condemning them to a slow death.

When buying plants, choose those grown without **neonicotinoids**. These insecticides are systemics, which mean that the poison enters every part of the plant including the nectar and pollen, making them potentially toxic to pollinators. Because of this they have been banned in some countries.

Native plants will, of course, attract certain insects that, in turn, will provide food for birds and other animals. That means that leaf damage is both expected and good—it's not the sign of a failed garden. In terms of the kind of pest infestation that wipes out large chunks of plant material, native plants will have greater resistance than exotics, especially if they're not given overly rich soil. Fertilized plants have been found to be more attractive to insects than those not fertilized.

Below: Native plants such as Carolina phlox generally come with built-in disease resistance.

Plant Diseases

Wetter, warmer weather is expected to favor many plant diseases, and certain cold-sensitive plant pathogens may now be able to overwinter. The first and best way to reduce or even eliminate the need for toxic fungicides is to choose disease-resistant plants suited to your soil type, preferably native, and plant them in the correct locations in the garden. Determine whether your plants need full sun, part sun, dappled shade, or deep shade so that they can grow robustly and take advantage of their built-in disease-fighting mechanisms. Plants that don't get their needs met in terms of sunlight, moisture, and soil conditions will be more susceptible to diseases such as blight, mildew, rust, mosaic viruses, and leaf spot.

When resorting to the use of fungicides, look for those that are guaranteed safe for bees. One option is to spray with a mineral-based horticultural oil, which will control some of the insects that spread diseases—aphids, whiteflies, thrips, and mites, for example. Fungicides labeled as organic may contain copper, sulfur, pyrethrin, or neem-oil, all of which have been found to be harmful to beneficial insects including bees.

Synthetic Fertilizers

There are many reasons for us to stop using synthetic fertilizers.

→ Studies have shown that four to six tons of carbon are emitted into the air for every ton of synthetic nitrogen fertilizer produced, meaning that the manufacturing process itself adds to global warming.

→ As we've seen earlier, one of the main goals of a climate-wise garden is to make it as low maintenance as possible. One great way to do this is to choose native plants that don't need fertilizing. In fact, applying synthetic fertilizers to native plants will often make them more prone to insect and disease attack and shorten their life-span. So the easy solution is to stop fertilizing.

→ Because the nutrients in synthetic fertilizers don't bind with organic matter in the soil, they leach into the groundwater and into local streams, rivers, and lakes. These leachates and the fertilizer runoff from heavy storms deplete oxygen in those bodies of water, killing fish and other wildlife. This leaching and runoff also leads farmers and home gardeners to compensate by applying even more fertilizer, creating a vicious cycle.

→ Often gardeners apply fertilizer in excess amounts, which leads to nitrous oxide emissions by soil microorganisms. The microorganisms in turn become overstimulated and end up digesting all of the good organic matter and leaving the soil depleted and nutrient poor. The soil, as a result, becomes more susceptible both to erosion and to compaction. Even more reason to give up our addiction to these products.

→ Lawns again: As a nation we dump a shocking amount of synthetic fertilizer onto our lawns to get them to perform the way we think they should. Reducing or eliminating the lawn is one answer; another is to spread a thin layer of compost on top of the lawn in spring and fall instead of using manufactured chemicals.

→ In the case of vegetables, fruits, and annuals, which need highly nutrient-rich soil, a more climate-friendly practice is to use organic fertilizers such as fish emulsion, liquid kelp, compost tea, worm castings, bone meal, cottonseed meal, soybean meal, alfalfa meal, mushroom compost, or bat guano. Adding one or more of these every four to six weeks will boost the health and productivity of these plants. These amendments help feed the plants and improve the soil structure without the introduction of toxic chemicals. Organic fertilizers contain humus, which sticks around longer in the soil and can restore a healthy microbe balance. A healthier soil leads to more plant resilience and better crop production.

Sweet Betsy trilliums and other woodland natives prefer rich, organic soil and need no synthetic fertilizers.

Gas-Powered Tools

The old standard practice of using gas-powered lawn mowers, leaf blowers, string trimmers, and leaf vacuums adds to global warming because of the CO_2 and other pollutants these machines emit. Unfortunately, millions of these pieces of equipment are still in use in the United States. The Environmental Protection Agency estimates that using a gas-powered lawn mower for one hour is equivalent to driving a car 200 miles. Pollution from running a leaf blower equates roughly to driving eleven newly manufactured cars for the same period of time. Manual tools powered by good old human muscle are, by far, the best option for reducing our carbon footprint. There are also electric, battery-powered, and solar-powered options available, which are quieter and much better for the environment than gas-powered models.

Plastic Pots and Garden Waste

When collecting yard waste, the most climate-friendly option is to use it for your own composting or place it in paper bags designed for this purpose rather than using plastic lawn and leaf bags. If you have a choice when buying plants, opt for those that come in biodegradable containers. If your plants come in plastic pots or six-packs, donate the containers to a school, nursery, or community garden or recycle them. Don't send them to the landfill.

CHAPTER NINE

Droughts, Floods, and the Wise Use of Water

> We understand that working with nature and not against it makes both environmental and economic sense.
>
> —Donald Harker,
> *Landscape Restoration Handbook*

CLIMATE CHANGE SHIFTS the gardener's relationship to water in two broad ways. On the one hand, longer, hotter summers with periods of drought mean that we have to reconsider how we're going to meet our garden's need for water as prudently as possible. On the other hand, more frequent and serious bouts of flooding due to hurricanes and other severe storms mean that we should be planning the garden layout to account for occasional periods of deluge.

More Frequent and Sustained Periods of Drought

The *National Climate Assessment* has predicted that, especially in the western part of the Southeast, water availability will decline in the coming decades. And in every part of the Southeast, longer, hotter summers and more frequent and longer periods of drought will mean more expensive water bills and potential losses of valued trees and other garden plantings unless we make some adjustments to business as usual. Check out the weekly, monthly, and seasonal drought projections from the National Oceanic and Atmospheric Administration at the U.S. Drought Monitor (www.climate.gov /maps-data/dataset/weekly-drought-map).

A heat wave is considered to be a period of a week or more with temperatures above 90 degrees. A drought is defined as an extended period of below-normal rainfall. During a heat wave, when the soil becomes overly dry, more sunlight is absorbed, causing both the soil and the air above it to get warmer, feeding a kind of vicious cycle. During a drought the soil often becomes hard and compacted, making it hard for roots to get the oxygen and water they need.

In addition to increasing ground-level ozone, which is a health risk to humans, higher temperatures can also harm plant life. Scientists have found that extreme heat events actually make a plant's working systems (photosynthesis and water transpiration) less efficient, so roots don't develop as strongly as they should and the plant's overall growth is harmed. When coupled with a period of drought, the higher air temperatures, higher soil temperatures, and insufficient water uptake can cause serious damage to plants.

Drought not only stresses plants by depriving them of needed water, but it makes them more vulnerable to insects and diseases and causes declines in a plant's growth rate and overall vigor. Roots fail to develop properly; beneficial soil organisms may be adversely affected; and in some cases the roots' hydraulic system fails. We now know that damage suffered from a drought can appear in trees as much as ten years later.

Trees and other plants communicate with one another when droughts occur, triggering a response to close the stomata (pores) on their leaves to retain water. But closed stomata mean lack of carbon uptake, which, if the drought lasts long enough, can eventually starve the plant to death. Trees and other plants can recover from drought damage if there are sufficiently favorable conditions and if those conditions occur soon enough and last long enough for the plant to repair itself.

In an area that's constantly exposed to wind, the soil will dry more quickly. Planting trees, hedges, tall ornamental grasses, or other windbreaks can reduce this drying-out effect. Light reflected from adjacent hard surfaces can also intensify the effects of a heat wave or drought. Heat- and drought-tolerant plants will fare better in these situations than those that need cooler, moister conditions.

Signs of heat stress and drought damage include leaves that are smaller than usual, wilt, turn brown or yellow, or fall off the plant. Leaf drop in trees that have been severely affected by drought generally starts at the center top of the canopy.

There are a number of simple steps we can take to minimize the risks of drought damage in our gardens, including hydrozoning, using drought-tolerant plants, planting in the fall, allowing for natural dormancy, avoiding practices that stress the plant further such as pruning or fertilizing during a drought, and conserving water by installing one or more rain barrels.

Below: Group plants according to their water needs. Smoke tree is among a large number of native trees that don't need constant irrigation.

HYDROZONING

Hydrozoning is the smart idea of grouping plants according to how much water they need in their native growing conditions. For example, plants such as blue flag iris (*Iris virginica*) and sensitive fern are found in soil that's almost constantly wet. Plants native to dry, rocky areas, such as butterfly weed, prefer soil that's somewhat moist but well drained or even dry. Certain sun-loving, drought-tolerant plants such as Spanish bayonet (*Yucca aloifolia*) will actually rot out unless they have well-drained soil. And there are many plants that fall in the middle.

The best gardening practice, whether you plan to water by hand or install an automatic irrigation system, is to group your plants according to their watering needs. Ideally you want to choose a majority of plants that need no supplemental watering at all. Those that need irrigation once or twice a month should be grouped together. Container plants, some annuals, and vegetables that need more frequent attention can be grouped in their own hydrozone. When you do irrigate, do it slowly and deeply so that the water can penetrate the deeper root zones. Shallow watering encourages shallow root growth.

Low areas that flood temporarily during storms will generally be moister even if the soil is loose and sandy. Such an area would be an excellent spot for deep-rooted plants that can tolerate standing water.

IRRIGATION

Of course, sufficient water is essential to the survival of any plant, and even a completely native garden will require some supplemental irrigation—especially during periods of prolonged drought. With that in mind, focusing on smart irrigation practices is an important part of climate-friendly gardening. Also, keep in mind that extreme drought may mean that all outdoor irrigation will be banned.

As discussed earlier, the U.S. Department of Agriculture estimates that almost half of all residential water use in the United States goes to irrigating lawns and gardens—and it's an even higher percentage in drier climates. Evaporation, wind, and runoff steal up to 50 percent of this irrigation. Especially during times of drought, when water resources are stressed, this amount of water usage is unsustainable. Further, treating and pumping the water that reaches us via our taps and garden hoses often involves burning fossil fuels and adds to the emission of greenhouse gases.

Although drip irrigation, which delivers water directly to the plant's root zone, is more efficient than overhead watering, some researchers have found that drought-tolerant plants, and native plants in general, don't do well on a steady diet of drip irrigation. They found that although the plants will grow lush, they'll also be more susceptible to a variety of diseases and will tend to die prematurely. For this reason, it's best to limit drip irrigation to vegetable gardens and to those natives whose natural habitats are riverbanks and wet spaces, those that tolerate occasional flooding, or those that can stand very poor drainage.

If you install an automatic irrigation system, there are climate-friendly considerations. First, and most obvious, is not to run the system when there's already been adequate rainfall. Rain-sensing systems will automatically cancel the next scheduled irrigation cycle when rainfall has been sufficient.

Another climate-friendly practice is to direct irrigation to only those plants that need it, not to every plant in the garden. The spray pattern should be designed so that water isn't wasted on driveways and other impermeable surfaces.

Even though watering slowly and deeply is important in order to encourage plant roots to dig deeper into the ground, some shallow surface watering will be of help in cooling the soil and easing plant stress during times of extreme heat or drought.

During a period of drought it's important to prioritize your watering so that the most vulnerable plants get first dibs. This includes newly planted trees and shrubs, any specimen plant that's of special value to you, and any other plants that haven't yet become firmly established. A gardener may have to face the reality that some plants—such as seedlings or other plants with newborn root systems—may not make it through a drought.

Below: Many native vines, including this bright orange trumpet creeper, stand up well to heat and drought.

DROUGHT DORMANCY

Many native plants have a built-in system for dealing with drought, which is to go temporarily dormant. The plants' stomata close up to preserve moisture, and they no longer put out lush, new growth. They no longer flower and set seed; they no longer increase in size by underground rhizomes or aboveground stolons. They just stay put and wait it out. This temporary dormancy should be respected rather than challenged, which is what happens when we overwater, fertilize, and encourage new unsupportable growth.

Incorporating as many drought-tolerant natives as possible in the garden means adjusting our expectations about what we need plants to do for us. Can we see dormancy as a remarkable example of nature's ingenuity and appreciate the fact that our plants are taking care of themselves in their own way? When conditions are favorable again, the dormant plants will perk up and look more vibrant.

FORGOING FERTILIZING AND COSMETIC PRUNING DURING A DROUGHT

If your area is experiencing extreme heat or drought, forgo pruning (except for diseased, damaged, or dead plant tissue). Pruning stimulates the growth of new stems and foliage and discourages root growth. Strong roots, of course, are especially important in surviving drought, so pruning can actually diminish the plant's drought resilience. Fertilizing also stimulates leaf growth, which simply stresses the drought-weakened plant even further because its roots can't keep up with the demand. Synthetic fertilizers are a particularly bad idea during a drought because they leach salts, which can burn the already dry plant roots.

HYDROPHOBIA

Sustained drought can lead to a problem called hydrophobia, which may sound like a psychological disorder but is actually a soil condition in which the top layer becomes impermeable to water, forming a kind of tough crust. This can happen with container plants as well as those planted in beds.

Mixing four teaspoons of a mild dish soap in a gallon of water and pouring this on the soil acts as a wetting agent and helps break through the crust, allowing you to deeply water the area afterward. The best solution is to prevent the soil from becoming so deeply dried out in the first place by monitoring the garden bed or container regularly.

DROUGHT-TOLERANT PLANTS

Drought-tolerant plants have adapted in various ways to deal with extreme heat. Some, such as white sage (*Artemisia ludoviciana*) and silverleaf mountain

Drought-Tolerant Native Grasses

Big bluestem (*Andropogon gerardii*)

Bitter panic grass (*Panicum amarum*)

Bottlebrush grass (*Elymus hystrix*)

Broom sedge (*Andropogon virginicus*)

Northern sea oats (*Chasmanthium latifolium*)

Pink muhly grass (*Muhlenbergia capillaris*)

Purple love grass (*Eragrostis spectabilis*)

Purple muhly grass (*Muhlenbergia sericea*)

Splitbeard bluestem (*Andropogon ternarius*)

Sugarcane plume grass (*Saccharum giganteum*)

Switch grass (*Panicum virgatum*)

Naturally drought-tolerant native fringe trees provide fruits for birds and small mammals and are covered in sumptuous blooms in spring.

mint (*Pycnanthemum incanum*), are coved in tiny insulating hairs. Succulents such as the eastern prickly-pear cactus (*Opuntia humifusa*) store water in their roots or trunks. Drought tolerance may also be indicated by threadlike foliage, which reduces surface area for water loss, as seen in common yarrow (*Achillea millefolium*) or threadleaf coreopsis (*Coreopsis verticillata*). These types of plants have built-in adaptability to extreme heat and drought.

There are dozens of native trees, shrubs, perennials, vines, and groundcovers that can withstand periods of drought (see appendix for details). The most drought-tolerant lawn grasses are Bermuda grass and zoysia grass. An excellent idea for drought-prone areas is the use of native ornamental grasses. They make beautiful additions to the garden, especially when planted in broad swaths.

ESTABLISHING STRONG PLANTS

Even though a plant is labeled drought tolerant, it still needs help from the gardener. When first planted, drought-tolerant species need to be watered and cared for like any other plant until they've established a strong root system. Infrequent deep watering will encourage deeper roots and more drought tolerance than frequent shallow watering. After becoming well established, these drought-tolerant plants should be allowed to follow their own instincts during periods of drought, with minimum watering. Give trees and shrubs top priority for watering during the first two years in their new locations until they develop sufficient root systems.

In the Mountains area of the Southeast, fall droughts are especially dangerous for evergreens such as pine, spruce, rhododendron, and boxwood, which won't be able to pull up any more water once the ground freezes. Give these plants at least one inch of water per week during fall drought conditions.

Grouping plants in natural communities or assemblages increases their drought tolerance. This includes planting trees in groups; as we're now learning, they're able to communicate with one another through underground networks, share resources, and signal impending dangers from drought, insect attack, and disease.

As we've already seen, plant-covered soil has a rich biological life, giving it better water retention and making it less susceptible to runoff than bare soil—important considerations for withstanding drought.

Slow-release watering bags, sometimes called camel bags, which wrap around the trunk of newly planted trees and shrubs, are useful in delivering water slowly and consistently. Some tree experts advise gardeners to use these only for a few months after first installing a new plant, to avoid the danger that roots will develop in a constricted fashion rather than spreading out and down.

PLANT IN THE FALL

Where extreme heat and drought from climate change are likely to be a problem—especially in the Coastal Plain and Piedmont areas—plants stand a better chance of survival if they've developed strong root systems. In these more heat-wave-prone areas of the Southeast, trees, shrubs, perennials, ferns, and ornamental grasses planted in the fall tend to have better drought tolerance than those planted in the spring or summer. Fall planting gives them a longer period of fairly mild weather with adequate moisture to establish a strong root system.

RAINWATER HARVESTING

One way to conserve water during periods of less-than-adequate rainfall is to install rain barrels to catch the natural runoff from downspouts. Water from rain barrels doesn't contain the added chemicals we get from our house-sourced water. It's better for plants because it doesn't kill microbes with water purifiers, and it's more climate friendly because it isn't dependent on energy the way tap water is. However, water from rain barrels is *not* safe to drink.

Rainwater harvesting lessens the amount of polluted runoff ending up in our streams, lakes, and ocean; it eases the demand on municipal water use; and once you set up your rain barrel, it's virtually free. Many states and municipalities encourage rainwater harvesting and provide information on their websites.

The cost and complexity of setting up a rain barrel ranges from minimal DIY construction to more sophisticated and expensive solutions. The basic idea is to divert water from the downspout leading off a roof gutter and into the mouth of a large container that's been equipped with a spigot. The top of the container should be covered with wire mesh or other type of fine filter to keep out debris and discourage mosquito breeding.

Rain barrels conserve water and are especially valuable during extended droughts.

Because rain barrels fill up quickly, it's important to provide for overflow either through a simple opening near the top of the barrel or a diverter designed for this purpose. The rain barrel should be elevated on blocks or a platform that's at least high enough to allow a watering can underneath.

Getting sufficient water pressure to run a hose from the rain barrel will depend on how full the container is, how high up it sits, and whether you've installed a pump. A series of rain barrels captures more water and provides more of a buffer in times of drought.

STEPS TO FOLLOW AFTER AN EXTENDED DROUGHT

1. Drought-stressed plants are vulnerable to disease and pest damage. Monitor your plants during and after a drought to catch these issues as early as possible.

2. Don't prune immediately after a drought except to remove dead or diseased plant material. Allow the plant time to recover.

3. Don't overwater. Accustom your plants to increased amounts of water gradually.

4. Don't fertilize drought-stressed plants.

5. Be aware that symptoms of drought damage may appear months or even years later.

Flooding

During the space of one growing season, gardeners in the Southeast may be faced not only with periods of drought but with episodes of severe storm flooding as well. In 2017, Hurricane Harvey dumped over fifty inches of rain on southeast Texas. Floods in Missouri, Mississippi, and Arkansas caused $20 million in damage in 2019. The frequency of flash floods and lowland flooding especially are expected to increase.

Flooding leads to soil erosion and excess runoff into nearby waterways. When the top layer of healthy soil is removed, plants are left with a nutrient-poor subsoil that often won't support plant life. Our natural wetlands absorb excess rainwater and are especially invaluable during these extreme weather events. This is why there's a strong focus on preserving them rather than draining and building on them.

Facing page:
Flooding in the Southeast is expected to increase with climate change. Plants native to wetlands will have good resistance to flood conditions.

Trees, shrubs, and other plants suffer from flooding in a number of ways. The empty soil pores that they normally use to take up oxygen are flooded, basically drowning the plant. In addition, harmful ethanol and hydrogen sulfide can build up in waterlogged soil; roots may be exposed; the storm may deposit a harmful layer of silt, virtually smothering the foliage and preventing transpiration; and the soil pH may be significantly altered, making it harder for the plant to take up vital nutrients.

Plants affected by flooding may show symptoms of yellowing or wilting leaves, smaller-than-normal new leaf growth, delayed leafing-out, or branch dieback. In many cases gardeners won't know the full extent of the damage for months and, in some cases, years. Planning ahead can mitigate the damage. Again, there are a few key takeaway points: lawn reduction, flood-tolerant plants, bioswales, raised beds, and rain gardens. We can also keep impervious surfaces to a minimum, using permeable materials for hardscaping whenever possible.

EXAMINE YOUR SPACE

During the next heavy rain, put on your galoshes and examine which parts of your yard are absorbing the water and which parts are pooling; the latter might be lower-lying areas or those next to lawns or hardscape elements. Hurricanes, unfortunately, provide an excellent opportunity to see just how much water will accumulate on which part of your landscape and for how many hours or days.

In heavy storms, water from gutters and downspouts can pour out so quickly and furiously that the ground doesn't have the time or absorptive ability to soak it all up. The excess runoff can carry harmful pollutants including trash, heavy metals, and bacteria into nearby storm drains and waterways; pollutants include not only pesticides and herbicides but, even if you garden organically, excess organic matter and eroded soil. An excellent solution for dealing with frequently flooded areas in your yard is to create a bioswale (see below).

Here are some further tips for dealing with potential flooding:

→ **Reduce your lawn size.** Lawns are very poor at absorbing water, which means that areas with large stretches of lawn will experience more runoff and more standing water than those with no or smaller lawn areas.

→ **Cover the ground with plants.** Covering the soil with plants works to mitigate not only drought conditions but also flooding, because bare soil promotes runoff and erosion.

→ **Create raised beds.** If you know that your area may be subject to flooding, consider installing raised beds for your more vulnerable plants such as vegetables, herbs, fruits, and other plants that can't withstand waterlogged soil.

→ **Choose flood-tolerant plants.** Many plants can recover from several feet of standing water that remains for hours or days. In cases of hurricanes, however, water may stand for weeks afterward, and only the most water-tolerant plants may survive (assuming that their foliage isn't completely submerged).

EXAMPLES OF FLOOD-TOLERANT PLANTS

If you have an area of the landscape that tends toward periodic wetness, you might choose native wetland species and plants whose native habitats include pocosins, swamps, or the edges of rivers and lakes, especially in situations where you know that a storm may leave weeks of standing water.

STEPS TO FOLLOW AFTER A SERIOUS FLOOD EVENT

1. **Stay out of floodwater.** It may be contaminated with health-threatening bacteria, viruses, and parasites. Wear protective clothing when cleaning up after a flood.

Native Trees That Tolerate Standing Water

Bald cypress (*Taxodium distichum*)

Pond cypress (*Taxodium ascendens*)

River birch (*Betula nigra*)

Southern wax myrtle (*Myrica cerifera*)

Swamp bay (*Persea palustris*)

Swamp cedar (*Thuja occidentalis*)

Swamp chestnut oak (*Quercus michauxii*)

Sweetgum (*Liquidambar styraciflua*)

Titi (*Cyrilla racemiflora*)

Water oak (*Quercus nigra*)

Water tupelo (*Nyssa aquatica*)

Native Shrubs That Tolerate Standing Water

Coastal witch alder (*Fothergilla gardenii*)

Inkberry (*Ilex glabra*)

Northern bayberry (*Myrica pensylvanica*)

Rose mallow (*Hibiscus moscheutos*)

Spicebush (*Lindera benzoin*)

Swamp azalea (*Rhododendron viscosum*)

Swamp rose mallow (*Hibiscus grandiflorus*)

Native rose mallow is one of many excellent flood-tolerant plants.

2. Before making any decisions about trees and other flood-damaged plants, wait a couple of months or more to see if they recover.

3. Wait until the soil dries out before walking on it or digging in it to avoid compaction.

4. Downed tree and limb removal can cause serious injuries. It may pay to call in an expert.

5. If plants have been inundated with salt water, rinse them off unless there's been sufficient rain.

6. Don't use a pressure washer to remove silt from plants. Spray water to rinse it off as soon as possible. Don't use soap or detergents on plants—it compromises the waxy cuticle.

7. Don't fertilize after a flood, because many plants will go naturally dormant at this time.

8. Check the stability of trees, especially newly planted ones. Cover exposed roots with organic matter.

9. Don't prune the first year after a flood except to remove dead, diseased, or broken branches.

10. If you have an area of turfgrass that's covered with debris, wait until the area has dried out, and then remove as much debris as possible and aerate it.

FRENCH DRAINS, DRY WELLS, AND BIOSWALES

The Environmental Protection Agency now considers storm-water runoff to be America's biggest non-point-source pollution problem. Gardeners can mitigate this problem through various forms of drainage engineering. The idea behind each of these constructions is to reshape the land to slow down the surge of heavy rainwater, allowing the ground time to absorb and filter it.

The first step, in each case, is to locate dips and low spots in your yard where water has a tendency to pool after a storm. Areas next to lawns, sidewalks, driveways, patios, roofs, and other low-permeability surfaces are often good candidates.

French drain. To install a French drain, (1) dig a trench one to two feet deep parallel to the major source of runoff; (2) line the trench with heavy-duty geotextile fabric; (3) put down a layer of gravel or recycled concrete pebbles; (4) place perforated PVC piping the length of the trench; (5) cover piping with gravel or recycled concrete pebbles; (6) cover with additional geotextile fabric; and (7) backfill with dirt. The water will seep into the perforated piping and be directed out to a drier area of the yard.

Dry well. A dry well is something like a vertical French drain. It can be located about ten feet away from a major downspout and connected via PVC piping in order to direct water away from the house, or it can be located in another area of the yard subject to flooding. Although there are more complex methods of creating a dry well, a simple way involves these basic steps: (1) dig a hole about three feet deep and four feet in diameter; (2) line it with geotextile cloth; (3) fill it with rocks, coarse gravel, or recycled concrete pebbles; (4) cover the rocks with additional geotextile fabric; and (5) backfill with soil. As with a French drain, a dry well buys time for excess runoff to percolate into the ground, where pollutants can be filtered out.

Bioswale. A bioswale is another way to slow water down, this time by inviting it to meander down from a higher to a lower grade and possibly around obstacles such as bio-logs (biodegradable coir logs) or rocks, following a curved path to another, drier part of the yard. Vegetation planted along a bioswale will also help with water absorption. Bioswales follow similar design instructions as rain gardens but tend to be shallower. They can be planted or filled with rocks.

RAIN GARDENS

Another option for capturing excess storm runoff and mitigating flood-prone areas of the yard is to create a rain garden. It should be located at least ten feet from the building foundation, ideally in a low-lying area prone to flooding or an area adjacent to impervious surfaces where the soil normally doesn't have time to absorb storm-water runoff.

The size of the rain garden should be in proportion to the square footage of the impervious surfaces that are going to drain into it. If your soil has a high clay content you may want to create a larger rain garden (60 percent of the impervious square footage). For sandy soil 30 percent may be large enough. But even a small rain garden, 5–10 percent of the impermeable square footage, will be of benefit. Choose a site that gets five or more hours of sun each day, if possible, and a site that's away from underground utility lines, heavy tree roots, or a septic field.

The depth of the rain garden will depend on how fast the site drains. Perform the drainage test described in chapter 7 and use that score to determine how many inches deep to dig (e.g., soil that drains at six inches per hour means a six-inch-deep hole; eight inches per hour means an eight-inch-deep hole). The depression you create might be circular or kidney shaped with sloping sides. If you surround it with a raised berm you'll provide additional growing space for plants that need better drainage. If it's built on a slope, a rain garden will benefit from a berm on the downhill side to prevent erosion.

Below: Native joe-pye weed can stand occasional wet feet and is a good choice for a rain garden. It attracts pollinators such as this monarch butterfly and provides seeds for songbirds.

Choose deep-rooted native plants that tolerate occasional flooding but don't need constant moisture. Plant directly in your native soil or create a mixture of 50 percent sand, 25 percent topsoil, and 25 percent compost. This may be the best bet if your soil has a particularly high clay content. Reliable, efficient drainage is the key to a successful rain garden.

You can use a rock-lined bioswale or a buried four-inch PVC pipe to direct storm water into the rain garden. Add a rock barrier where the water enters the rain garden to slow it down and prevent soil erosion. Rain gardens are designed to be dry most of the time and to absorb storm-water flooding within twelve to forty-eight hours. They don't hold standing water long enough to allow mosquitoes to breed.

Median Strip Plantings

If your garden is limited to the median strip between the sidewalk and the street, you can still create a beautiful, small bit of landscaping—with the added benefit that you'll be uplifting the spirits of everyone who walks by. You'll also be helping to prevent runoff, filter rainwater, and mitigate the urban heat island effect. Be aware that these hell strips, as they're sometimes called, belong to the city or county. Check to see if there are any regulations in place.

Because there's generally no built-in source of irrigation for median strips, it's best to choose sturdy, drought-tolerant plants and those that can withstand urban conditions such as pollution and road salt. Choosing native plants, of course, will benefit native wildlife and attract the pollinators and beneficial insects that improve the health of the local ecosystem.

Even when you've selected drought-tolerant plants, it's important to consistently bring water out to the median strip when you first plant it, until the plants establish strong root systems and can fend for themselves.

You may want to edge your space with bricks or other materials or outline the beds with low, wicket-style barriers to keep out foot traffic. Include stepping stones for people to walk from their cars to the sidewalk. Be aware that dogs, pedestrians, bicyclists, and others may occasionally invade your median strip garden and plant accordingly. Consider making a tapestry

Median strip gardens are a great way to capture runoff and attract pollinators. Planting in galvanized steel containers with holes punched in the bottom allows you to create your own soil mix.

of low-growing native groundcovers or incorporating low-growing native shrubs with native perennials and grasses.

Designing a median strip garden is similar to designing a backyard garden in many ways. First, get to know your site. Are there overhead wires that would limit the height of any tree you might want to plant? Are there underground wires, gas lines, or other utility considerations? How much sun or shade does the area get, and what's the soil like? Does it tend to stay baking-hot dry, or does it pool and flood during heavy downpours? If it's a flood-prone area, you might consider turning all or part of it into a rain garden.

Perforated tin washtubs or other recycled containers can be filled with an organic growing medium in areas where tree roots dominate and where direct planting in the ground might be difficult. When planting directly in compacted soil, you can aerate it with a pitchfork. Spreading a layer of leaf mold or other organic compost on top will also help speed the development of healthy soil.

CHAPTER TEN

Growing Food

This intersection of food and climate is a place where we can exercise our decision-making power and engage in meaningful action, every time we eat or work in the garden.

—Green America

G ROWING YOUR OWN FOOD is one of the great joys of gardening. Not only does it provide a healthy source of nourishment, but it saves money, sequesters carbon in the ground, cuts back on the carbon footprint of food transportation, and brings great satisfaction in a relatively short period of time. Where an oak tree might take several decades to mature, you can plant radish seeds and expect to bite into the peppery pink-and-white globes within six to ten weeks. With canning and freezing, you can preserve fresh vegetables, fruits, and herbs to enjoy throughout the year. And growing food is a great way to teach children about the wonders of gardening.

Planting vegetables, fruit trees, and berry bushes increases biodiversity —one of the key goals of climate-friendly gardening. The pollen and nectar of the flowers will attract beneficial bees, wasps, and beetles. The foliage of peas, beans, and many herbs provides larval food for a variety of butterflies. Caterpillars and pollinator insects, in turn, attract songbirds, toads, and small mammals. Birds and small mammals benefit from the fruits and berries as well.

Farmers who grow monocultures rely heavily on synthetic fertilizers. They routinely dig up the soil with mechanical tillers and create conditions favorable to wind and water erosion. These practices add to global warming by releasing greenhouse gases—accounting for a significant part of the problem worldwide. What's called regenerative farming, on the other hand, can sequester carbon and improve crop resilience at the same time. Many of the principles focus on the health of the soil. These include employing low- or no-till planting practices, covering the soil with organic compost, growing cover crops, and using crop rotation so that rich, healthy soil produces greater and healthier crop yields while avoiding the ecological damage caused by traditional farming practices. As home gardeners, we can adopt these same regenerative farming practices in growing fruits and vegetables.

Vegetables

WARM-WEATHER VEGETABLES

Warm-weather vegetables need warm soil in order to start off well, which is why they aren't planted in the garden until after the frost-free date in the spring. This date varies widely depending on where you're gardening. In Lafayette, Louisiana, for example, it occurs near the end of February; in Roanoke, Virginia, it's normally the first week of May. Check with your local agricultural extension service to determine your date. Warm-weather vegetables may continue bearing throughout the summer and into fall, depending on where you live and whether the plants are subject to heat waves (temperatures in the mid- to upper nineties), which may cause them to stop bearing.

Start peppers, eggplants, and tomatoes indoors six to eight weeks before the frost-free date in your growing area.

Some warm-weather vegetables—such as cucumbers, squash, okra, sweet potatoes, corn, and melons—can be sown directly in the ground. Others such as eggplants, tomatoes, and peppers are best started indoors six to eight weeks before the frost-free date, hardened off (acclimated to outdoor conditions), and then transplanted into the garden. Warm-weather vegetables need six to ten hours of full sun each day. They benefit from a thick layer of mulch and attention to keeping the soil evenly moist. Harvesting regularly and applying an organic fertilizer will help keep the plants producing.

Summer heat and diseases can make growing tomatoes particularly challenging for southeastern gardeners. Tomato seedlings should be planted in enriched organic soil as soon as the ground warms. Choosing disease-resistant and early varieties or grafted plants, planting deeply, and using containers or raised beds will help your chances of success.

COOL-WEATHER VEGETABLES

Cooler weather provides southeastern gardeners the opportunity to grow a wide variety of additional vegetables. In the Piedmont and Coastal Plain areas, **leafy greens** such as Swiss chard, lettuce, spinach, arugula, and other salad greens (as well as herbs such as parsley and dill) can be sown directly in the soil in the late summer and early fall for harvesting in winter and spring. Fall planting has the advantage of warm soil, cool temperatures, and fewer pests. If you miss the fall planting season these leafy greens can be started instead in early spring. Once the weather becomes hot, most of these greens will set flower, or "bolt," and lose their sweet flavor. The exception is Swiss chard, which generally stands up better to hot summer weather. In the Mountains area, leafy greens are sown in March and April for spring/summer harvesting and again in August for fall harvesting.

Cole crops include broccoli, cauliflower, Brussels sprouts, kale, collards, mustard, kohlrabi, and cabbage. Like other cool-weather vegetables, in the Coastal Plain and Piedmont they can be planted out in late winter/early spring for a springtime/early summer harvest and again in early fall for a fall/winter/spring harvest. In the Mountains, cole crops are planted in cool spring weather and again in July and August in order to harvest the vegetables before danger of a hard freeze.

Cool-season **root vegetables** include carrots, turnips, beets, potatoes, shallots, onions, radishes, and rutabagas. Planting times are late winter/early spring and then again late summer and fall. Root vegetables don't transplant well, so direct sowing is best. In the coldest parts of the Southeast, root crops should be covered with a heavy protective mulch to prevent freezing, or they should be harvested before the ground freezes. Garlic is one root vegetable that has its own calendar: plant it in the fall and harvest it the following summer. One warm-season root vegetable, the sweet potato, is planted after the frost-free date in spring and harvested during the summer like its warm-season companions.

Most **beans and peas**, except for bush and dwarf varieties, will need some sort of a support—a trellis, stakes, or a tepee structure. In the Coastal Plain and Piedmont, English or garden peas—as well as sugar snaps and snow peas—can be treated like other cool-weather vegetables with a late winter/early spring planting and another in the late summer/fall for harvesting during the subsequent cool months. In the Mountains the second planting occurs in July and August for harvesting before a hard freeze. Southern peas are planted later in the season and stand up better to hot weather. Some heat-tolerant varieties of pole beans will continue producing throughout the summer months.

SEASON EXTENSION STRATEGIES

There are several ways to extend the growing season, especially for those in the Mountains area experiencing longer and colder winter weather.

Row covers. Reusable fabric rolls are cut to your garden bed length and supported by metal hoops. The covers float above the crops, insulating them from the cold. For the coldest weather, use several layers.

Straw bales. A rectangle of straw bales arranged on the outside of a garden bed and topped by old window frames will act like a mini greenhouse, providing insulation against winter weather. These are excellent for starting spring vegetables. Prop up the window frames to provide ventilation on warm days so the plants don't get overheated.

Cold frames. These are constructed from wood or plastic for the siding with old window frames or other types of glass on top.

High and low tunnels. Made of galvanized steel tubes, wood, and plastic, tunnels come in a variety of heights and lengths and serve as unheated greenhouses for growing crops in cold weather and for starting seedlings. Tunnels can give the gardener access to fresh food year-round.

Planning out your vegetable garden on paper ahead of time is helpful so that you can maximize your growing space (planting both vertically and horizontally, for example) and so you'll have a timeline for seed germination and vegetable ripening. Planning for the height, spread, and other growth habits of your vegetables will help you orchestrate the many factors at play and allow each plant to have enough sunlight and growing space to stay healthy.

Choose vegetable varieties that are listed as disease and pest resistant. In the hottest parts of the Southeast, gardeners should consider varieties that mature early in order to avoid the height of pest and disease season. Check with your local agricultural extension service for varieties that have been proven to do well in your area and for the recommended planting windows for each vegetable, and think about planting every few weeks within that window to get a succession of crop yields.

Include some interplanting with annuals and perennials. This will help attract the beneficial insects that prey on vegetable pests such as cutworms, aphids, and scales and will benefit pollen-dependent vegetables such as squash, melons, eggplants, and others.

As part of your planning, decide in advance how you'll rotate vegetables each year from one planting bed to a different one—a very important practice for garden health. Follow heavy feeders such as corn, tomatoes, beets, and cabbage with legumes (such as alfalfa, clover, beans, and peas), which will renew the soil's nitrogen and compensate for soil depletion. Rotating planting beds minimizes the chances that pests attracted to certain vegetables, such as squash borers or cucumber beetles, will take up residence year after year in the same squash or cucumber patch.

Warm-weather vegetables need six to ten hours of sun each day and consistent watering from rain, hand watering, or irrigation (an inch per week). Many cool-weather vegetables including cole crops, root vegetables, and leafy greens can get by with three to six hours of direct sun or a full day's worth of dappled shade. Under these conditions they'll usually take longer to mature and may produce smaller heads. The advantages of partial shade are that it lessens the impact of extreme summer heat and slows the bolting process, and it gives the gardener some flexibility if a full-sun location isn't available.

Facing page:
Warm-weather vegetables such as okra—as well as squash, peppers, melons, corn, eggplants, and tomatoes—need a minimum of six hours of full sun in order to produce well.

SOIL FOR VEGETABLES

Because vegetables need to germinate, flower, and produce within a relatively short time frame, they have different cultural needs than other plants in the garden. For this reason, raised beds or containers with rich, organic soil work well. Ideal soil for vegetables contains 5–8 percent organic matter and has a loose enough texture to allow for good drainage. It's also dense enough to allow for water absorption and retention. Combining about 50 percent topsoil with 50 percent organic matter (large amounts of garden compost, aged shredded leaves, and well-aged poultry or cow manures together with smaller amounts of worm castings, mushroom compost, or shredded bark) will create a rich soil suitable for high-yield vegetable production.

SHEET COMPOSTING, OR LASAGNA GARDENING

The layered, or "lasagna," garden (a term coined by garden writer Patricia Lanza in her book *Lasagna Gardening: A New Layering System for Bountiful Gardens*) is a climate-friendly way to compost in place and create rich soil especially appropriate for growing vegetables. Begin by outlining an area of the garden that hasn't yet been planted— or if you plan to have a raised bed, construct the frame. Next put down a layer of newspaper to discourage weeds, and wet it thoroughly. After this, pile on alternate layers of brown and green materials (see compost section in chapter 7), using a ratio of two or three parts brown to one part green, until the layers are about twelve to eighteen inches high (or possibly quite a bit taller depending on what organic material you have on hand). Adding a final layer of topsoil or mulch will help weigh the pile down to keep materials from blowing off at first.

Below: Building raised beds is one way to provide rich, organic soil for vegetables.

Keep the lasagna bed moist but not sopping wet. It can take anywhere from several months to a year for the materials to decompose into rich organic soil. The process will be somewhat quicker if the materials are finely chopped beforehand, the weather is warm, the bed is in full sun, and you incorporate generous amounts of aged manure into the green layers.

COVER CROPS/GREEN MANURE

If you've got a sunny area of the garden you're not currently using but plan to convert to a vegetable bed, or possibly a vegetable patch that you've just finished harvesting, it's a good idea to plant it with a cover crop of legumes such as peas, beans, red clover, hairy vetch, or alfalfa, which will stabilize the soil and fix nitrogen, making it available to whatever you plant next in that space. Sometimes called "green manure," these cover crops reduce the need for fertilizers. They also prevent erosion and runoff, improve soil structure, benefit soil organisms, and attract pollinators. Other cover crops such as winter wheat, oats, or winter rye, which don't fix nitrogen, will still benefit the soil by sequestering carbon, stabilizing the soil, and preventing erosion from wind and water.

Winter cover crops are specifically planted after the harvesting of summer crops, to benefit the soil until the next spring's planting season. Recommended planting windows for winter cover crops are mid-August to mid-September in the Mountains, late August to mid-October in the Piedmont, and September and October in the Coastal Plain. Cut down your cover crop a couple of weeks before the frost-free date in spring and three to four weeks before you plan to plant something else in that spot. This will give the cover crop clippings and residue time to decompose and form a beneficial mulch.

Fruits

Almost all fruits and fruiting trees need a minimum of six hours of direct sunlight a day during the growing season and attention to watering during periods of drought in order to thrive and bear fruit. Unfortunately, there are some favorite fruits and fruit trees that *can* be successfully grown in the

Southeast but only with a fairly rigorous program of spraying for pests and diseases. This makes them not ideal for a climate-friendly garden. These include apples, peaches, pears, plums, persimmons, and strawberries. Growing the most disease-resistant variety of these fruits—and making sure the variety is suited to your particular growing zone—may cut down somewhat on the need for toxic chemicals.

Better yet, consider the many great fruits we can grow without the need for spraying. Native rabbiteye blueberry (*Vaccinium ashei*) is an excellent choice for Coastal Plain and Piedmont gardens; be sure to plant more than one variety with the same bloom time in order to get cross-pollination and fruiting. Native highbush blueberry (*Vaccinium corymbosum*) will thrive in all parts of the Southeast including the Mountains area, as will dwarf huckleberry (*Gaylussacia dumosa*). Muscadine grapes (*Vitis rotundifolia*) are natives with built-in disease and insect resistance and are best suited to the Coastal Plain and Piedmont areas—grow them on a strong support.

Black raspberry (*Rubus occidentalis*) and red raspberry (*Rubus idaeus*) will grow and spread vigorously in all parts of the Southeast, although they may die out after about seven years due to a common virus. Some forms are erect and arching and some trail on the ground. You may want to prune them to waist height to avoid flopping, but be aware that fruiting occurs on "old wood," meaning on the stems and canes from the previous year's growth, not on this year's new growth.

Pawpaw trees (*Asimina triloba*), sometimes called Appalachian bananas, produce large, tropical-flavored fruits with a custardy texture. For best results, plant two or three separate varieties no farther than thirty feet apart.

Beautiful flowering mayhaw trees (*Crataegus opaca*) bear fruit in late spring. The fruit looks like small crabapples, has a tart bite, and is valued for use in jams and jellies. The native red

Below: Black raspberries are among many native fruits that provide wildlife benefits.

mulberry (*Morus rubra*) is another lovely ornamental tree that bears abundant fruit in spring. Native elderberry bushes (*Sambucus nigra*) produce large, showy flowers in summer and plentiful dark berries at summer's end. Unlike most other fruits, elderberries prefer some dappled sunlight and cooler temperatures.

For gardeners in the coastal Southeast, nonnative loquats (*Eriobotrya japonica*) are handsome flowering trees with the bonus of abundant fruit. Two nonnative citrus fruits for the Coastal Plain area, satsuma oranges (*Citrus unshiu*) and kumquats (*Citrus japonica*), are cold-hardy as well. Figs (*Ficus carica*), which are not native, will do well in the Coastal Plain and Piedmont areas—but be careful not to buy the California variety, which require a specific pollinator not present in the Southeast.

Some fruits are *not* generally recommended for the Southeast because of the extreme heat of our summers (apricots and rhubarb), the fact that our winters are not frost free (avocados, pineapples, limes, and many citrus fruits), and disease and pest problems (apricots and cherries). Nonnative hardy bananas grow very well for us in most areas of the Southeast and add dramatic foliage to the garden, but they generally won't bear fruit because they need a fourteen-month frost-free stretch to do so.

Chapter 8 contains information about organic fertilizers and organic pest and disease control, all of which is applicable to growing vegetables and fruits.

White and purple phlox mixed with purple coneflowers make a beautiful garden while enriching the local ecosystem at the same time.

CHAPTER ELEVEN

Make It a Community Affair

Ultimately, failure to halt global warming will mean that the world we leave for our children and grandchildren will be vastly less supportive of the people, plants and wildlife than the one we cherish today.

—National Wildlife Federation, *The Gardener's Guide to Global Warming*

MAYBE YOU'RE IN LOVE with the idea of gardening but you don't have a patch of dirt to call your own. Or you do have a garden, but you want to do even more to contribute to climate-friendly gardening in your area. There are excellent opportunities nearby.

Get Involved with Schools, Churches, and Other Local Groups

If you're a parent or a teacher, or if you know someone connected with a school, creating a rain garden, butterfly garden, or raised-bed vegetable garden can be a wonderful project. These school gardens provide the kind of hands-on learning that will connect youngsters with the natural world in a way that may set each of them on their own path toward climate-friendly gardening for the rest of their lives.

Gardens adjacent to places of worship offer another possibility for learning, sharing, and fellowship while helping to mitigate climate change. These gardens, especially if they involve growing food, can also connect the congregation with the local neighborhood and provide help for those living in food deserts.

If your city or town has a community garden, signing up for your own plot is a great way to be outdoors, grow your own produce and flowers, meet other gardeners, and get tips on what plants do best in your part of the state. Starting a community garden from scratch may require talking to local officials and community leaders to find an unused piece of land. This is doable by anyone with a little persistence. In Wilmington, North Carolina, one lone individual initiated eight community gardens, which are now flourishing in vacant lots, on hospital grounds, at low-income housing sites, in churchyards, at an elementary school, at a recreation club for at-risk teens, and at a neighborhood civic club. This was all done through networking with local community leaders, civic groups who could provide volunteer labor, and garden centers willing to help out with materials and through sheer, unbridled enthusiasm.

Get together a group in your neighborhood or school to "adopt" a species of songbird, butterfly, or other animal, learning what plants they need for shelter, food, and reproduction, and find ways to bring more of those plants into your community.

You can have your garden qualified as a Certified Wildlife Habitat by the National Wildlife Federation (see www.nwf.org/garden-for-wildlife/certify) or, on a larger scale, have your entire neighborhood, town, or city certified as a Community Wildlife Habitat (see www.nwf.org/communitywildlifehabitat).

Work with Local Government

To bring more native plants to your community, you can talk to your elected officials about possible volunteer beautification projects along median strips, in parks, and along roadside margins. See if you can get your city recognized as part of Tree City USA (see www.arborday.org/programs /treecityusa) or Bee City USA (see www.beecityusa.org). In some cases, states have created wild-flower routes, which attract tourism in addition to bene-fiting the environment.

Speak to your local transportation department about creating a roadside mowing policy that allows pollinator-friendly plants to remain unmowed all summer, with one late mowing in October.

Read up on the "sponge city" movement, an effort to incorporate green infrastructure by making pavement more permeable, planting trees, using green roofs and green walls, and encouraging new and existing structures to incorporate energy-saving, climate-friendly features. A sponge city suffers less from the urban heat island effect, enjoys cooler and cleaner air, is better able to capture and filter storm-water runoff, and saves on energy costs. And, as we all know, the positive mental and emotional benefits of urban green spaces shouldn't be underestimated.

Volunteer

Get involved with your local land conservation group protecting open spaces and natural areas within your town and in adjacent counties. See if the group needs volunteer help removing invasives from natural habitats or rescuing native plants. Along the coast, there are shoreline restoration projects that need volunteer help. Your local arboretum or public garden may also have a program using volunteers to maintain the gardens or to lead docent tours teaching the public about the value of native plants.

In the Southeast there are joint government and private efforts under way to save natural grasslands, such as the Southeast Grasslands Initiative and the Piedmont Prairie Partnership (www.segrasslands.org).

There are also initiatives to save plant species that have traditionally been important to Native American peoples, such as the Culturally Signif-icant Plant Species Initiative (www.cherokeenaturalresources.com/cspsi).

Ecologists are working to help relocate endangered plant species that, for various reasons, will be unable to migrate to suitable new areas on their own. Species are chosen carefully to ensure that they won't become invasive in their new location or carry pathogens or insects. Check to see if there's a plant relocation project nearby that needs volunteer help.

Seed banking—collecting seeds from straight native species—is another effort worth getting involved with.

Become a Citizen Scientist

Visit Nature's Notebook (www.usanpn.org/natures_notebook) to see what the USA National Phenology Network is doing to develop models for plant and animal survival with the help of citizen scientists who help track leaf emergence and other seasonal events in plant and animal species. You can become one of these citizen scientists.

Either on your own or with friends, neighbors, or your child's school, join Budburst (budburst.org) and help scientists track things such as the timing of natural events in the garden (flowering, fruiting, arrival of various pollinators) or the effectiveness of different nativars in attracting pollinators. Budburst can suggest ways for you to help assess the impacts of climate change all year.

An app on your smartphone lets you join in the World Bee Count project (www.beescount.org) by taking pictures of insects you see on flowers and sending them in.

Make Small Efforts That Add Up

→ Take the Pollinator Protection Pledge (www.xerces.org/bring -back-the-pollinators).

→ Keep notes on whether the nativars you plant are attracting pollinators.

→ When you shop at local nurseries or large gardening centers, put in a plug with management about carrying more native plants.

CHAPTER TWELVE

Learn More about Climate Change Gardening

Like it or not, and prepared or not, we are the mind and stewards of the living world. Our own ultimate future depends on that understanding.

—E. O. Wilson, *Half Earth*

WORKING IN THE GARDEN can be a balm for the spirit, a healthy exercise for the body, and a source of great satisfaction. The more time we spend tending to our plants and watching the bees nuzzling into pollen-filled flower cups, the more we want to know about how it all works. There's no end to what we can learn about plants and the wildlife that depends on them. Below are some resources to check out, both for your own geographical area and for more general information on gardening and climate change.

State-by-State Resources

Publication dates for individual articles are given if available; all websites and online databases were most recently accessed in 2021.

ALABAMA

Alabama Plant Atlas. www.floraofalabama.org.

Alabama Wildflower Society. www.alwildflowers.org.

Hansen, Curtis. "Wildflowers of Alabama." In *Encyclopedia of Alabama.* November 6, 2009. www.encyclopediaofalabama.org/article/h-2482.

Lady Bird Johnson Wildflower Center. "Special Collections: Alabama Recommended." www.wildflower.org/collections/collection.php ?collection=AL.

PlantNative. "Native Plant List for Georgia, Alabama and Mississippi." www.plantnative.org/rpl-algams.htm.

Sierra Club. "Climate Change in Alabama." www.sierraclub.org/alabama /climate.

ARKANSAS

Arkansas Native Plant Society. www.anps.org.

City of Fayetteville, Arkansas. "Climate Change in Arkansas." https://www .fayetteville-ar.gov/3282/Climate-Change-in-Arkansas.

Climate Change in Arkansas. Norman, Okla.: Southern Climate Impacts Planning Program, 2014. http://www.southernclimate.org/documents /climatechange_arkansas.pdf.

Fowler, Allison, and Jane Anderson, eds. "Climate Change in Arkansas." Section 7 of *Arkansas Wildlife Action Plan: Designing a Future for Arkansas Wildlife.* Rev. ed. Little Rock: Arkansas Game and Fish Commission, 2015. https://www.wildlifearkansas.com/materials/2017/01 %20Introduction.pdf.

Klingman, Gerald. "Plant of the Week: New USDA Plant-Hardiness Zone Map." University of Arkansas Division of Agriculture Research and Extension, 2012. www.uaex.edu/yard-garden/resource-library/plant -week/hardiness-zone-map-2-17-12.aspx.

Lady Bird Johnson Wildflower Center. "Special Collections: Arkansas Recommended." www.wildflower.org/collections/collection.php ?collection=AR.

PlantNative. "Native Plant List for Arkansas, Louisiana, Eastern Oklahoma, and Eastern Texas." www.plantnative.org/rpl-arla.htm.

What Climate Change Means for Arkansas. Washington, D.C.: U.S. Environmental Protection Agency, 2016. 19january2017snapshot.epa.gov/sites /production/files/2016-09/documents/climate-change-ar.pdf.

FLORIDA (NORTHERN)

Florida Association of Native Nurseries. www.plantrealflorida.org.

Florida Climate Center. "Climate Change." https://climatecenter.fsu.edu /topics/climate-change.

Florida Energy and Climate Commission. *The Effects of Climate Change on Florida's Ocean and Coastal Resources.* Tallahassee: Florida Oceans and Climate Council, 2009. www.floridadep.gov/rcp/rcp/documents/effects-climate -change-floridas-ocean-and-coastal-resources.

Florida Native Plant Society. www.fnps.org.

Florida Wildflower Foundation. https://flawildflowers.org.

Florida Wildflowers Growers Cooperative. www.floridawildflowers.com.

Lady Bird Johnson Wildflower Center. "Special Collections: North Florida Recommended." www.wildflower.org/collections/collection.php ?collection=FL_north.

What Climate Change Means for Florida. Washington, D.C.: U.S. Environmetal Protection Agency, 2016. www.epa.gov/sites/production/files/2016-08 /documents/climate-change-fl.pdf.

GEORGIA

Georgia Climate Project. www.georgiaclimateproject.org.

Georgia Conservancy. www.georgiaconservancy.org/policies/climate.

Georgia Department of Natural Resources. "Plants That Attract Georgia Wildlife." https://georgiawildlife.com/planting-flowers-yourself -and-birds.

Georgia Native Plant Society. www.gnps.org.

Lady Bird Johnson Wildflower Center. "Special Collections: Georgia Recommended." www.wildflower.org/collections/collection.php ?collection=GA.

PlantNative. "Native Plant List for Georgia, Alabama and Mississippi." www.plantnative.org/rpl-algams.htm.

Wade, Gary, Elaine Nash, Ed McDowell, Brenda Beckham, and Sharlys Crisafulli. *The Complete Guide to Native Plants for Georgia*. Athens: University of Georgia Extension, 2008. https://secure.caes.uga.edu/extension /publications/files/pdf/B%20987_11.PDF.

KENTUCKY

Colangelo, Rachel. "What Climate Change Means for Kentucky." *Louisville Cardinal*, November 7, 2018. https://www.louisvillecardinal.com/2018/11 /what-climate-change-means-for-kentucky.

Kentucky Climate Center. www.kyclimate.org.

Kentucky Native Plant Society. www.knps.org.

Lady Bird Johnson Wildflower Center. "Special Collections: Kentucky Recommended." www.wildflower.org/collections/collection.php ?collection=KY.

PlantNative. "Native Plant List: Kentucky and Tennessee." www.plant native.org/rpl-kytn.htm.

Spence, Carol Lea. "Kentucky Climate Consortium Empowers Kentuckians to be Environmental Stewards." *UKnow*, January 28, 2020. https://uknow .uky.edu/research/kentucky-climate-consortium-empowers-kentuckians -be-environmental-stewards.

LOUISIANA

Lady Bird Johnson Wildflower Center. "Special Collections: Louisiana Recommended." www.wildflower.org/collections/collection.php ?collection=LA.

Louisiana Native Plant Society. https://www.facebook.com/Louisiana NativePlantSociety.

PlantNative. "Native Plant List for Arkansas, Louisiana, Eastern Oklahoma, and Eastern Texas." www.plantnative.org/rpl-arla.htm.

U.S. Geological Survey. "Guide to the Plants of Louisiana." https://warcapps.usgs.gov/PlantID.

MISSISSIPPI

Lady Bird Johnson Wildflower Center. "Special Collections: Mississippi Recommended." www.wildflower.org/collections/collection.php?collection=MS.

Mississippi Native Plant Society. www.mississippinativeplantsociety.org.

Mississippi State University Extension. "Native Shrubs for Mississippi Landscapes." www.extension.msstate.edu/native-shrubs-for-mississippi-landscapes.

PlantNative. "Native Plant List for Georgia, Alabama and Mississippi." www.plantnative.org/rpl-algams.htm.

University of Mississippi. "Native Mississippi Plants." www.olemiss.edu/depts/landscape/nativeplants.html.

NORTH CAROLINA

Audubon North Carolina. "700 Bird-Friendly Native Plants for North Carolina." nc.audubon.org/700.

Climate Risk and Resilience Assessment Plan. Raleigh: North Carolina Department of Environmental Quality, 2020. https://files.nc.gov/ncdeq/climate-change/resilience-plan/2020-Climate-Risk-Assessment-and-Resilience-Plan.pdf.

Lady Bird Johnson Wildflower Center. "Special Collections: North Carolina Recommended." www.wildflower.org/collections/collection.php?collection=NC.

North Carolina Native Plant Society. www.ncwildflower.org.

North Carolina State Extension Service. "North Carolina Extension Gardener Plant Toolbox." plants.ces.ncsu.edu.

Sea Grant North Carolina. "Coastal Landscapes." https://ncseagrant.ncsu.edu/program-areas/healthy-ecosystems/coastal-landscapes.

SOUTH CAROLINA

Lady Bird Johnson Wildflower Center. "Special Collections: South Carolina Recommended." www.wildflower.org/collections/collection.php?collection=SC.

South Carolina Native Plant Society. www.scnps.org.

South Carolina Wildlife Federation. www.scwf.org.

University of South Carolina A. C. Moore Herbarium. "South Carolina Plant Atlas." http://herbarium.biol.sc.edu/scplantatlas.html.

TENNESSEE

Lady Bird Johnson Wildflower Center. "Special Collections: Tennessee Recommended." www.wildflower.org/collections/collection.php?collection=TN.

PlantNative. "Native Plant List: Kentucky and Tennessee." www.plantnative.org/rpl-kytn.htm.

Tennessee Invasive Plant Council. www.tnipc.org.

Tennessee Native Plant Society. www.tnps.org.

TEXAS (EASTERN)

Lady Bird Johnson Wildflower Center. "Special Collections: Texas East Recommended." www.wildflower.org/collections/collection.php?collection=TX_east.

Native Plant Society of Texas. https://npsot.org/wp.

PlantNative. "Native Plant List for Arkansas, Louisiana, Eastern Oklahoma, and Eastern Texas." www.plantnative.org/rpl-arla.htm.

Texas SmartScape. Plant database. www.txsmartscape.com/plant-search/list.php.

VIRGINIA

Lady Bird Johnson Wildflower Center. "Special Collections: Virginia Recommended." www.wildflower.org/collections/collection.php?collection=VA.

Native Plants for Northern Virginia. Northern Virginia: Plant NoVa Natives Campaign, 2014. www.novaregion.org/DocumentCenter/View/10615 /Northern-Virginia-Native-Plant-Guide—-FINAL?bidId.

Plant Virginia Natives. www.plantvirginianatives.org.

Virginia Department of Conservation and Recreation. "Native Plants for Conservation, Recreation and Landscaping." www.dcr.virginia.gov /natural-heritage/nativeplants.

Virginia Native Plant Society. www.vnps.org.

WEST VIRGINIA

Lady Bird Johnson Wildflower Center. "Special Collections: West Virginia Recommended." www.wildflower.org/collections/collection.php ?collection=WV.

PlantNative. "Native Plant List: Maryland, Virginia, and West Virginia." www.plantnative.org/rpl-mdvawv.htm.

West Virginia Native Plant Society. www.wvnps.org.

Recommended Reading

Beck, Travis. *Principles of Ecological Landscape Design*. Washington, D.C.: Island, 2013.

Bormann, F. Herbert, Diana Balmori, and Gordon T. Geballe. *Redesigning the American Lawn: A Search for Environmental Harmony*. New Haven, Conn.: Yale University Press, 2001.

Carson, Rachel. *Silent Spring*. 1962. Reprint, New York: Houghton Mifflin, 2002.

Christopher, Thomas. *The New American Landscape: Leading Voices on the Future of Sustainable Gardening*. Portland, Ore.: Timber, 2011.

Darke, Rick, and Douglas W. Tallamy. *The Living Landscape*. Portland, Ore.: Timber, 2014.

Deppe, Carol. *The Resilient Gardener*. White River Junction, Vt.: Chelsea Green, 2010.

Druse, Ken. *The New Shade Garden: Creating a Lush Oasis in the Age of Climate Change*. New York: Harry N. Abrams, 2019.

Filippi, Olivier. *The Dry Gardening Handbook: Plants and Practices for a Changing Climate*. London: Thames and Hudson, 2008.

Harker, Donald, Sherri Evans, Marc Evans, and Kay Harker. *Landscape Restoration Handbook*. Boca Raton, La.: Lewis, 1993.

Henson, Robert. *The Thinking Person's Guide to Climate Change*. Boston: American Meteorological Association, 2019.

Hosier, Paul. *Seacoast Plants of the Carolinas*. Chapel Hill: University of North Carolina Press, 2018.

Kolbert, Elizabeth. *The Sixth Extinction: An Unnatural History*. New York: Henry Holt, 2014.

Lanza, Patricia. *Lasagna Gardening: A New Layering System for Bountiful Gardens*. Emmaus, Pa.: Rodale, 1998.

McKibben, Bill. *Eaarth: Making a Life on a Tough New Planet*. New York: Henry Holt, 2010.

———. *The End of Nature*. New York: Anchor, 1989.

Mellichamp, Larry. *Native Plants of the Southeast: A Comprehensive Guide to the Best 460 Species for the Garden*. Portland, Ore.: Timber, 2014.

Packard, Stephen, and Cornelia F. Mutel. *The Tallgrass Restoration Handbook*. Washington, D.C.: Island, 2005.

Porcher, Richard, and Douglas Rayner. *A Guide to the Wildflowers of South Carolina*. Columbia: University of South Carolina Press, 2001.

Rainer, Thomas, and Claudia West. *Planting in a Post-wild World*. Portland, Ore.: Timber, 2015.

Reed, Sue, and Ginny Stibolt. *Climate-Wise Landscaping: Practical Actions for a Sustainable Future*. Gabriola Island, B.C.: New Society, 2018.

Soleri, Daniela, David A. Cleveland, and Stephen E. Smith. *Food Gardens for a Changing World*. Wallingford, UK: Center for Agriculture and Bioscience International, 2019.

Solomon, Steve. *Gardening When It Counts: Growing Food in Hard Times*. Gabriola Island, B.C.: New Society, 2006.

Spira, Timothy. *Wildflower and Plant Communities of the Southern Appalachian Mountains and Piedmont*. Chapel Hill: University of North Carolina Press, 2011.

Tallamy, Douglas W. *Bringing Nature Home: How You Can Sustain Wildlife with Native Plants*. Portland, Ore.: Timber, 2007.

————. *Nature's Best Hope: A New Approach to Conservation That Starts in Your Yard*. Portland, Ore.: Timber, 2019.

Vogt, Benjamin. *A New Garden Ethic: Cultivating Defiant Compassion for an Uncertain Future*. Gabriola Island, B.C.: New Society, 2017.

Wallace-Wells, David. *The Uninhabitable Earth: Life after Warming*. New York: Tim Duggan Books, 2019.

Weaner, Larry, and Thomas Christopher. *Garden Revolution: How Our Landscapes Can Be a Source of Environmental Change*. Portland, Ore.: Timber, 2016.

Wilson, Edward O. *Half Earth: Our Planet's Fight for Life*. New York: Liveright, 2016.

Online Sources on Climate Change Gardening

Publication dates for individual articles are given if available; all websites and online databases were most recently accessed in 2021.

Antonelli, Alexandre, ed. *State of the World's Plants and Fungi*. Richmond, UK: Royal Botanic Gardens, Kew, 2020. www.kew.org/sites/default/files /2020-10/State%20of%20the%20Worlds%20Plants%20and%20Fungi %202020.pdf.

Arbor Day Foundation. "Hardiness Zone Map." 2015. www.arborday.org /media/zones.cfm.

————. "Tree City USA." www.arborday.org/programs/treecityusa.

Audubon Society. "Native Plants Database." www.audubon.org/native -plants.

Bee City USA. www.beecityusa.org.

Biota of North America Program. "BONAP's North American Plant Atlas." 2015. http://bonap.net/napa.

Budburst. budburst.org.

Candeias, Matt. *In Defense of Plants* (podcast). www.indefenseofplants.com /podcast.

Center for Plant Conservation. https://saveplants.org.

"The Climate-Friendly Gardener: A Guide to Combating Global Warming from the Ground Up." *Union of Concerned Scientists*, April 3, 2012. www.ucsusa.org/resources/climate-friendly-gardener.

Cornell Institute for Climate Smart Solutions. https://ecommons.cornell.edu/handle/1813/52051.

Eastern Band of Cherokee Indians. "Culturally Significant Plant Species Initiative." https://cherokeenaturalresources.com/cspsi.

Fourth National Climate Assessment. Vol. 2, *Impacts, Risks, and Adaptation in the United States.* Washington, D.C.: U.S. Global Change Research Program, 2018. https://nca2018.globalchange.gov.

Glick, Patty, ed. *The Gardener's Guide to Global Warming: Challenges and Solutions.* Reston, Va.: National Wildlife Federation, 2007. www.nwf.org/~/media/PDFs/Global-Warming/GardenersGuideToGlobalWarming.ashx.

Green America. "Climate Victory Gardens." www.greenamerica.org/climate-victory-gardens.

Grow Appalachia. www.growappalachia.berea.edu.

Longleaf Alliance. www.longleafalliance.org.

Lowe, Andrew. "How Do We Keep Gardening in the Face of Climate Change?" *Conversation*, February 23, 2017. www.theconversation.com/how-do-we-keep-gardening-in-the-face-of-a-changing-climate-72647.

NASA Global Precipitation Measurement Mission. "Global Climate Change: Vital Signs of the Planet." https://gpm.nasa.gov/education/websites/global-climate-change-vital-signs-planet.

National Oceanic and Atmospheric Administration. "Weekly Drought Map." www.climate.gov/maps-data/dataset/weekly-drought-map.

National Wildlife Federation. "Certify Your Habitat." www.nwf.org/garden-for-wildlife/certify.

———. "Garden for Wildlife." www.nwf.org/Garden-for-Wildlife.

———. "Native Plant Finder." www.nwf.org/nativeplantfinder.

Nature's Notebook. "Become an Observer Today in 3 Steps." www.usanpn.org/natures_notebook.

New York Botanical Garden. "Gardening in a Changing Climate." April 2021. www.libguides.nybg.org/changingclimate.

Southeastern Grasslands Initiative. www.segrasslands.org.

We are Nature's stewards.

Stibolt, Ginny. *Green Gardening Matters*. www.greengardeningmatters
.blogspot.com.

University of Maryland Extension. "Adapting Your Garden to the Impacts
of Climate Change." Updated September 24, 2021. https://extension
.umd.edu/resource/adapting-your-garden-impacts-climate-change.

U.S. Department of Agriculture, Natural Resources Conservation Service.
"Plants Database." https://plants.usda.gov/home.

U.S. Environmental Protection Agency. "Ecoregions." www.epa.gov/eco
-research/ecoregions.

U.S. Forest Service. "Climate Change Atlas: Tree Atlas." https://www.fs.fed
    .us/nrs/atlas/tree.

Westlake, Meryl. "Plants in the Earth's Sixth Extinction." Royal Botanic
    Gardens, Kew, June 10, 2019. www.kew.org/read-and-watch/plants
    -sixth-extinction.

World Bee Count Project. "Global Pollinator Map." www.beescount.org.

Xerces Society. "Bring Back the Pollinators." www.xerces.org/bring-back
    -the-pollinators.

APPENDIX

Key to Chart Symbols

SUNLIGHT PREFERENCE

F   Full sun six or more hours a day

PS   Shade for part of the day or constant dappled sunlight. (Note that morning sun with afternoon shade is gentler on plants that can't tolerate full sun.)

S   Deep shade

SOIL PREFERENCE

W   Tolerates occasional short periods of wet soil

M   Well-drained moist soil

D   Fast-draining dry soil

SOUTHEAST REGION SUITABILITY

M   Mountains

P   Piedmont

C   Coastal Plain

Drought-Tolerant Native Trees for Southeastern Landscapes

The following trees must be watered and cared for until they are well established. Once they've established a strong root system, they can withstand periods of drought but may need supplemental watering if the period of drought is extensive.

PLANT NAME Latin name	Common name	USDA ZONE	SUNLIGHT	SOIL	SOUTHEAST REGION
SMALL TREES (up to 30 feet tall)					
Acer saccharum subsp. *leucoderme*	chalk maple	5–9	F/PS/S	M	MP
Chionanthus virginicus	fringe tree	3–9	F/PS	M	MPC
Cotinus obovatus	American smoke tree	4–8	F/PS	M-D	MPC
Crataegus marshallii	parsley hawthorn	7–9	F/PS/S	W-M-D	PC
Crataegus phaenopyrum	Washington hawthorn	4–8	F/PS	M-D	MPC
Crataegus viridis	green hawthorn	4–8	F	M-D	MPC
Cyrilla racemiflora	titi	5–11	F/PS	W-M	PC
Frangula caroliniana	Carolina buckthorn	5–9	F/PS	M-D	MPC
Ilex vomitoria	yaupon holly	7–9	F/PS/S	W-M-D	PC
Morus rubra	red mulberry	4–9	F/PS	M-D	MPC
Myrica cerifera	southern wax myrtle	7–11	F/PS/S	W-M-D	MPC
MEDIUM TREES (30–50 feet tall)					
Acer pensylvanicum	striped maple	3–7	PS/S	M	MP
Cladrastis kentukea	yellowwood	4–8	F/PS	M	MP
Ilex opaca	American holly	5–9	F/PS/S	M-D	MPC
Juniperus virginiana	eastern red cedar	3–9	F/PS	M-D	MPC
Ostrya virginiana	American hop hornbeam	3–9	F/PS/S	M-D	MPC
Prunus caroliniana	Carolina cherry laurel	7–10	F/PS	M	PC
Sassafras albidum	sassafras	4–9	F/PS	M-D	MPC
Thuja occidentalis	eastern arborvitae	2–7	F/PS	W-M-D	M

PLANT NAME *Latin name*	*Common name*	USDA ZONE	SUNLIGHT	SOIL	SOUTHEAST REGION
LARGE TREES (over 50 feet tall)					
Acer rubrum	red maple	2–9	F/PS	M	MPC
Betula nigra	river birch	3–9	F/PS	W-M	MPC
Carya glabra	pignut hickory	4–9	F/PS	M-D	MPC
Celtis laevigata	southern hackberry	5–10	F/PS	M-D	MPC
Diospyros virginiana	persimmon	4–9	F/PS	M-D	MPC
Gymnocladus dioicus	Kentucky coffee tree	3–8	F/PS	M-D	MP
Liquidambar styraciflua	sweetgum	5–9	F/PS	W-M-D	MPC
Nyssa sylvatica	blackgum	3–9	F/PS	W-M-D	MPC
Pinus palustris	longleaf pine	7–9	F	M-D	PC
Pinus rigida	pitch pine	4–7	F/PS	M-D	MPC
Platanus occidentalis	American sycamore	4–9	FPS	W-M-D	MPC
Quercus alba	white oak	3–8	F/PS	M-D	MPC
Quercus geminata	sand live oak	7–10	F/PS	W-M-D	C
Quercus laurifolia	laurel oak	7–9	F/PS	W-M	PC
Quercus macrocarpa	bur oak	2–8	F/PS	M-D	M
Quercus montana	chestnut oak	4–8	F/PS	M-D	MPC
Quercus muehlenbergii	chinquapin oak	3–7	F	M-D	MP
Quercus rubra	northern red oak	3–8	F/PS	M	MPC
Quercus shumardii	Shumard oak	5–9	F/PS	W-M-D	MPC
Quercus stellata	post oak	5–9	F	M-D	MP
Quercus texana	Nuttall oak	6–9	F	W-M-D	MPC
Quercus virginiana	live oak	8–10	F/PS	M-D	C
Tilia americana	American linden	4–8	F/PS	M-D	MPC
Ulmus alata	winged elm	6–9	F/PS	M-D	MPC

Drought-Tolerant Native Shrubs for Southeastern Landscapes

The following shrubs must be watered and cared for until they are well established. Once they've established a strong root system, they can withstand periods of drought but may need supplemental watering if the period of drought is extensive.

PLANT NAME *Latin name*	*Common name*	USDA ZONE	SUNLIGHT	SOIL	SOUTHEAST REGION
Aesculus parviflora	bottlebrush buckeye	4–8	F/PS	M	MPC
Alnus serrulata	tag alder	4–9	F/PS	W-M	MPC
Amorpha fruticosa	indigo bush	3–9	F/PS	W-M	MPC
Aronia arbutifolia	red chokeberry	6–8	F/PS/S	W-M-D	MPC
Aronia melanocarpa	black chokeberry	3–8	F/PS	W-M-D	MP
Asimina parviflora	dwarf pawpaw	7–10	F/PS	M-D	PC
Baccharis halimifolia	groundsel bush	5–9	F/PS	W-M-D	MPC
Callicarpa americana	American beautyberry	6–10	F/PS/S	M-D	MPC
Calycanthus floridus	sweetshrub	4–9	F/PS/S	M-D	MPC
Cartrema americana	tea olive	6–9	F/PS/S	M-D	PC
Castanea pumila	Allegheny chinquapin	5–9	F/PS	M-D	MPC
Ceanothus americanus	New Jersey tea	4–8	F/PS	M-D	MPC
Ceratiola ericoides	Florida rosemary	8–10	F/PS	M-D	C
Clethra alnifolia	summersweet	3–9	F/PS/S	W-M	C
Clinopodium coccineum	scarlet wild basil	7–9	F/PS	D	PC
Comptonia peregrina	sweet fern	2–6	F/PS	M-D	MPC
Crataegus uniflora	dwarf hawthorn	4–9	F/PS	W-M-D	MPC
Diervilla sessilifolia	southern bush honeysuckle	4–8	F/PS	M-D	M
Euonymus americanus	hearts-a-bustin'	6–9	F/PS	M	MPC
Fothergilla gardenii	coastal witch alder	5–8	F/PS	W-M	C
Fothergilla latifolia	witch alder	4–8	F/PS	W-M	MP
Gaylussacia dumosa	dwarf huckleberry	5–9	F/PS	M-D	MPC

PLANT NAME *Latin name*	*Common name*	USDA ZONE	SUNLIGHT	SOIL	SOUTHEAST REGION
Hydrangea quercifolia	oakleaf hydrangea	5–9	F/PS	M	MPC
Hypericum tenuifolium	Atlantic St.-John's-wort	8–10	F/PS	M-D	C
Ilex verticillata	winterberry holly	3–9	F/PS/S	W-M-D	MPC
Ilex × attenuata 'Fosteri'	Foster's holly	7–9	F/PS	M-D	MPC
Ilex × attenuata 'Savannah'	Savannah holly	7–9	F/PS	M-D	MPC
Illicium floridanum	anise tree	7–10	PS/S	W-M-D	MPC
Illicium parviflorum	small anise tree	6–9	F/PS/S	W-M-D	MPC
Itea virginica	Virginia sweet spire	5–9	PS	W-M-D	MPC
Myrica cerifera	southern wax myrtle	7–9	F/PS	W-M-D	PC
Myrica pensylvanica	northern bayberry	3–7	F/PS	W-M-D	MPC
Opuntia humifusa	eastern prickly-pear cactus	7–10	F/PS	D	MPC
Philadelphus inodorus	Appalachian mock orange	5–10	F/PS	M-D	MPC
Physocarpus opulifolius	ninebark	2–8	PS/F	W-M-D	MP
Prunus angustifolia	Chickasaw plum	5–8	F	M-D	PC
Rhapidophyllum hystrix	needle palm	7–10	F/PS	W-M-D	C
Rhododendron austrinum	Florida flame azalea	7–9	PS	M-D	MPC
Rhododendron canescens	honeysuckle azalea	5–9	F/PS	W-M-D	MPC
Rhododendron periclymenoides	pinxter bloom azalea	4–9	F/PS	W-M	MPC
Rhus aromatica	fragrant sumac	3–9	F/PS	M-D	MPC
Rhus copallinum	winged sumac	4–9	F/PS	M-D	MPC
Rubus allegheniensis	Allegheny blackberry	3–8	F/PS	M-D	MPC
Sabal minor	dwarf palmetto	7–10	F/PS	W-M-D	PC
Sabal palmetto	cabbage palm	7–11	F	W-M-D	PC
Serenoa repens	saw palmetto	8–11	F/PS/S	W-M-D	PC
Symphoricarpos orbiculatus	coralberry	2–7	F/PS/S	M-D	MPC
Vaccinium arboreum	huckleberry	7–9	F/PS	M-D	MPC
Vaccinium pallidum	lowbush blueberry	5–9	F/PS	M-D	MPC

Drought-Tolerant Native Shrubs for Southeastern Landscapes (continued)

PLANT NAME Latin name	Common name	USDA ZONE	SUNLIGHT	SOIL	SOUTHEAST REGION
Viburnum dentatum	arrowwood viburnum	3–8	F/PS	M-D	MPC
Viburnum prunifolium	blackhaw viburnum	3–8	F/PS	M-D	MPC
Xanthorhiza simplicissima	yellowroot	3–9	PS	W-M-D	MPC
Yucca aloifolia	Spanish bayonet	6–11	F/PS	D	PC
Yucca filamentosa	Adam's needle	4–10	F/PS	M-D	MPC
Yucca gloriosa	Spanish dagger	7–11	F/PS	M-D	MPC
Zamia integrifolia	coontie	8–11	F/PS	M-D	C

Drought-Tolerant Native Perennials for Southeastern Landscapes

The following perennials must be watered and cared for until they are well established. Once they've established a strong root system, they can withstand periods of drought. However, if drought is prolonged they may need supplemental watering.

PLANT NAME Latin name	Common name	USDA ZONE	SUNLIGHT	SOIL	SOUTHEAST REGION
Achillea millefolium	common yarrow	3–9	F	M	MPC
Agave virginica	false aloe	6–9	F/PS	D	MPC
Allium cernuum	nodding onion	4–8	F/PS	M-D	MP
Amsonia tabernaemontana	eastern bluestar	3–9	F/PS	M	MPC
Armeria maritima	sea thrift	4–8	F/PS	M-D	MPC
Asclepias purpurascens	purple milkweed	3–8	F/PS	M-D	MPC
Asclepias syriaca	common milkweed	3–9	F	M-D	MPC
Asclepias tuberosa	butterfly weed	3–9	F/PS	M-D	MPC
Asclepias verticillata	whorled milkweed	4–9	F/PS	M-D	MPC
Baptisia alba	white wild indigo	5–8	F/PS	M-D	PC
Baptisia australis	blue false indigo	4–9	F/PS	W-M-D	MPC
Baptisia tinctoria	wild indigo	3–9	F/PS	M-D	MPC
Camassia scilloides	wild hyacinth	4–8	F/PS	M	PC
Chrysogonum virginianum	green-and-gold	6–8	PS/S	M	MPC
Chrysopsis mariana	Maryland golden aster	4–9	F/PS	M-D	MPC
Clinopodium carolinianum	Georgia basil	8–9	F/PS	D	PC
Conradina canescens	beach rosemary	8–10	F	D	C
Coreopsis grandiflora	large-flowered coreopsis	4–9	F/PS	D	MPC
Coreopsis lanceolata	lanceleaf coreopsis	4–9	F/PS	M-D	MPC
Coreopsis major	woodland coreopsis	5–9	F/PS	M-D	MPC
Coreopsis tripteris	tall coreopsis	3–8	F	M-D	MPC
Coreopsis verticillata	threadleaf coreopsis	3–9	F/PS	M-D	MPC
Dyschoriste oblongifolia	oblongleaf twinflower	7–10	F/PS	M-D	PC

Drought-Tolerant Native Perennials for Southeastern Landscapes (continued)

PLANT NAME Latin name	Common name	USDA ZONE	SUNLIGHT	SOIL	SOUTHEAST REGION
Echinacea pallida	pale purple coneflower	3–10	F/PS	M–D	MPC
Echinacea purpurea	purple coneflower	3–8	F/PS	MD	MPC
Erigeron pulchellus	robin's plantain	3–8	F/PS	M	MPC
Eryngium yuccifolium	rattlesnake master	5–9	F	D	MPC
Erythrina herbacea	coral bean	6–11	F/PS	M–D	C
Eurybia divaricata	white wood aster	3–8	PS/S	M–D	MPC
Eurybia macrophylla	bigleaf aster	3–8	PS/S	M–D	MPC
Gaillardia aestivalis	lanceleaf blanketflower	5–9	F	D	MPC
Gaillardia pulchella	beach blanketflower	2–11	F/PS	D	C
Geranium maculatum	wild geranium	3–11	F/PS	M	MP
Helianthus angustifolius	swamp sunflower	5–9	F/PS	W–M	MPC
Helianthus divaricatus	woodland sunflower	3–9	PS	M–D	MPC
Heliopsis helianthoides	false sunflower	3–9	F/PS	M–D	MPC
Heuchera americana	American alumroot	4–9	F/PS/S	M–D	MPC
Hypericum prolificum	shrubby St.-John's-wort	4–8	F/PS	M–D	MPC
Iris cristata	dwarf crested iris	3–9	PS	M–D	MPC
Liatris spicata	blazing star	3–8	F/PS	W–M–D	MPC
Lilium michauxii	Carolina lily	6–9	PS	M	MPC
Maianthemum racemosum	false Solomon's seal	4–8	PS	M	MPC
Monarda fistulosa	wild bergamot	3–9	F/PS	M–D	MP
Monarda punctata	spotted bee balm	3–9	F/PS	M–D	MPC
Oenothera fruticosa	sundrops	4–9	F/PS	M–D	MPC
Oenothera lindheimeri	gaura	5–9	F/PS	D	MPC
Oenothera speciosa	pink evening primrose	5–8	F/PS	M–D	MPC
Penstemon australis	southern beardtongue	5–9	F/PS	M–D	PC

PLANT NAME Latin name	Common name	USDA ZONE	SUNLIGHT	SOIL	SOUTHEAST REGION
Penstemon digitalis	white beardtongue	3–8	F	M-D	MP
Penstemon laevigatus	eastern smooth beardtongue	6–8	F/PS/S	M-D	MPC
Penstemon smallii	Small's beardtongue	5–8	F/PS	M-D	M
Phlox carolina	Carolina phlox	3–8	F/PS	W-M-D	MPC
Phlox stolonifera	creeping phlox	5–8	F/PS	M-D	MPC
Phlox subulata	moss phlox	3–9	F/PS	M-D	MPC
Podophyllum peltatum	mayapple	3–8	PS/S	W-M-D	MP
Polygonatum biflorum	Solomon's seal	3–9	PS/S	W-M-D	MPC
Prunella vulgaris	self-heal	3–9	F/PS	M	MPC
Pycnanthemum incanum	silverleaf mountain mint	4–8	F/PS	M-D	MP
Pycnanthemum tenuifolium	slender mountain mint	4–8	F/PS	W-M-D	MPC
Rudbeckia fulgida	black-eyed Susan	3–9	F	M-D	MPC
Rudbeckia hirta	gloriosa daisy	3–8	F/PS	M-D	MPC
Rudbeckia maxima	giant coneflower	4–9	F/PS	M-D	MPC
Rudbeckia subtomentosa	sweet coneflower	4–8	F/PS	M-D	MPC
Ruellia caroliniensis	Carolina wild petunia	6–11	PS	M-D	MPC
Salvia coccinea	scarlet sage	8–10	F/PS	M-D	PC
Salvia greggii	autumn sage	6–9	F/PS	M-D	MPC
Salvia lyrata	lyreleaf sage	5–8	F/PS/S	W-M-D	MPC
Scutellaria incana	downy skullcap	5–8	PS	M-D	MPC
Scutellaria serrata	showy skullcap	5–9	F/PS	M-D	MP
Sedum ternatum	mountain stonecrop	4–9	PS/S	M-D	MP
Silene caroliniana	Carolina campion	5–8	F/PS	M-D	MPC
Silene virginica	fire pink	4–8	F/PS	M-D	MPC
Solidago caesia	wreath goldenrod	4–8	F/PS	M-D	MPC
Solidago chilensis	licorice goldenrod	4–9	F/PS	M-D	MPC
Solidago rugosa	rough-stemmed goldenrod	4–8	F/PS	M-D	MPC

Drought-Tolerant Native Perennials for Southeastern Landscapes (*continued*)

PLANT NAME *Latin name*	*Common name*	USDA ZONE	SUNLIGHT	SOIL	SOUTHEAST REGION
Solidago sempervirens	seaside goldenrod	3–8	F	W-M-D	C
Solidago speciosa	showy goldenrod	3–8	F	M-D	MPC
Spigelia marilandica	Indian pink	5–9	PS	M	MPC
Stokesia laevis	Stokes' aster	5–9	F/PS	W-M	MPC
Symphyotrichum cordifolium	heart-leaved aster	3–8	F/PS	M	MPC
Symphyotrichum ericoides	downy aster	3–8	F/PS	M-D	MPC
Symphyotrichum georgianum	Georgia aster	3–9	F	M-D	MPC
Symphyotrichum laeve	smooth blue aster	4–8	F/PS	M-D	MPC
Symphyotrichum lateriflorum	calico aster	4–8	F/PS	M-D	MPC
Symphyotrichum novae-angliae	New England aster	4–8	F/PS	W-M-D	MP
Symphyotrichum oblongifolium	aromatic aster	3–8	F	M-D	MPC
Symphyotrichum patens	late purple aster	4–8	F/PS	M-D	MPC
Symphyotrichum pilosum	frost aster	4–8	F	M-D	MPC
Tradescantia ohiensis	smooth spiderwort	4–9	F/PS/S	W-M-D	MPC
Verbena canadensis	rose verbena	6–10	F/PS	M-D	MPC
Verbena stricta	hoary verbena	4–8	F	M-D	MPC
Vernonanthura nudiflora	sandhills ironweed	7–9	F/PS/S	M-D	C
Viola pedata	bird's-foot violet	4–8	F/PS	M	MPC
Zizia aurea	golden Alexander	3–8	F/PS	W-M-D	MPC

Other Drought-Tolerant Native Plants for Southeastern Landscapes

The following are excellent native ferns, ornamental grasses, groundcovers, and vines that will tolerate brief periods of drought. As with drought-tolerant trees and shrubs, these plants must be watered and cared for until they are well established. They may need supplemental watering if the period of drought is extensive.

PLANT NAME Latin name	Common name	USDA ZONE	SUNLIGHT	SOIL	SOUTHEAST REGION
FERNS					
Dennstaedtia punctilobula	hay-scented fern	3–7	F/PS/S	M-D	MPC
Dryopteris australis	Dixie wood fern	5–9	PS/S	W-M-D	C
Dryopteris intermedia	evergreen wood fern	3–8	PS/S	W-M	MPC
Hemionitis lanosa	woolly fern	5–8	F/PS	M-D	MPC
Homalosorus pycnocarpos	glade fern	3–8	PS/S	M	MPC
Osmunda claytoniana	interrupted fern	3–7	PS/S	W-M-D	MP
Polystichum acrostichoides	Christmas fern	3–9	PS/S	M-D	MPC
Thelypteris normalis	southern shield fern	7–10	PS/S	M-D	MPC
Woodwardia virginica	Virginia chain fern	4–10	F/PS/S	W-M-D	MPC
ORNAMENTAL GRASSES					
Andropogon gerardii	big bluestem	4–9	F	M-D	MPC
Andropogon ternarius	splitbeard bluestem	5–10	F/PS	M-D	MPC
Andropogon virginicus	broom sedge	3–9	F/PS	M-D	MPC
Chasmanthium latifolium	northern sea oats	5–9	F/PS	W-M-D	MPC
Deschampsia cespitosa	tufted hair grass	4–9	F/PS	W-M	MPC
Elymus hystrix	bottlebrush grass	5–8	PS/S	M-D	MP
Eragrostis spectabilis	purple love grass	5–9	F/PS	M-D	MPC
Muhlenbergia capillaris	pink muhly grass	5–9	F	M-D	MPC
Muhlenbergia sericea	purple muhly grass	8–11	F/PS	W-M	C
Panicum amarum	bitter panic grass	2–9	F	M-D	C
Panicum virgatum	switch grass	3–9	F/PS	W-M-D	MPC
Saccharum giganteum	sugarcane plume grass	4–10	F	W-M-D	MPC
Sorghastrum nutans	Indian grass	4–9	F	M-D	MPC

Other Drought-Tolerant Native Plants for Southeastern Landscapes (continued)

PLANT NAME Latin name	Common name	USDA ZONE	SUNLIGHT	SOIL	SOUTHEAST REGION
GRASSES USED AS LAWNS OR LAWN SUBSTITUTES					
Carex pensylvanica	Pennsylvania sedge	3–8	F/PS/S	M-D	MP
Muhlenbergia schreberi	nimble will	6–11	F/PS	M-D	MPC
Stenotaphrum secundatum	St. Augustine grass	8–10	F	M-D	C
GROUNDCOVERS					
Aristida stricta	Carolina wire grass	7–10	F/PS	W-M-D	PC
Berberis repens	creeping mahonia	4–9	F/PS/S	M-D	MPC
Calyptocarpus vialis	straggler daisy	8–10	F/PS/S	M-D	MPC
Carex laxiculmis	glaucous wood sedge	4–9	PS/S	W-M	MP
Chrysogonum virginianum	green-and-gold	6–8	PS/S	M	MPC
Erigeron pulchellus	robin's plantain	3–8	F/PS	M	MPC
Pachysandra procumbens	Allegheny spurge	5–9	PS/S	M	MPC
Phlox nivalis	trailing phlox	6–8	F/PS	M-D	MPC
Schizachyrium scoparium	little bluestem	3–10	F	W-M-D	MPC
Sedum ternatum	mountain stonecrop	4–9	PS/S	M-D	MP
Vaccinium crassifolium	creeping blueberry	6–9	F/PS	M-D	PC
Xanthorhiza simplicissima	yellowroot	3–9	PS	W-M-D	MPC
VINES					
Ampelaster carolinianus	climbing aster	6–9	F/PS	W-M-D	PC
Bignonia capreolata	cross vine	5–9	F/PS	W-M-D	MPC
Campsis radicans	trumpet creeper	4–10	F/PS	W-M-D	MPC
Gelsemium sempervirens	Carolina jessamine	6–10	F/PS	W-M-D	MPC
Lonicera sempervirens	coral honeysuckle	4–9	F/PS	W-M-D	MPC
Parthenocissus quinquefolia	Virginia creeper	4–10	F/PS	W-M-D	MPC
Passiflora incarnata	passionflower vine	5–9	F/PS	M-D	MPC
Vitis rotundifolia	muscadine grape	5–9	F/PS	W-M-D	MPC
Wisteria frutescens	American wisteria	5–9	F/PS	W-M-D	PC

Flood-Tolerant Native Trees for Southeastern Landscapes

The following trees can withstand short periods of inundation.
An asterisk * following the Latin name indicates the plant can grow
in soil that remains wet year round.

PLAN NAME Latin name	Common name	USDA ZONE	SUNLIGHT	SOIL	SOUTHEAST REGION
SMALL TREES (up to 30 feet tall)					
Aesculus pavia	red buckeye	4–8	F/PS	M-W	PC
Amelanchier arborea	downy serviceberry	4–9	F/PS	M	MPC
Amelanchier canadensis	eastern serviceberry	3–8	F/PS	M	PC
Carpinus caroliniana	American hornbeam	3–9	PS/S	W-D	MPC
Cornus amomum	silky dogwood	4–8	F/PS/S	W-M	MPC
Cornus foemina*	swamp dogwood	5–8	F/PS	W-M-D	MPC
Crataegus marshallii	parsley hawthorn	7–9	F/PS/S	W-M-D	PC
Cyrilla racemiflora*	titi	5–11	F/PS	W-M	PC
Ilex cassine	dahoon holly	7–9	F/PS	W-M	MPC
Ilex decidua	possumhaw	5–9	F/PS	W-M-D	PC
Ilex vomitoria	yaupon holly	7–9	F/PS/S	W-M-D	PC
Styrax americanus	American silverbell	6–8	F/PS	W-M	MPC
MEDIUM TREES (30–50 feet tall)					
Asimina triloba	pawpaw	5–9	F/PS/S	W-M	MPC
Chamaecyparis thyoides	Atlantic white cedar	3–9	F/PS	W-M	C
Crataegus aestivalis	mayhaw	4–8	F/PS	W-M	PC
Gordonia lasianthus*	loblolly bay	7–9	F/PS	W-M	C
Persea palustris*	swamp bay	7–11	F/PS	W-M-D	C
Prunus caroliniana	Carolina cherry laurel	7–10	F/PS	M	PC
Thuja occidentalis	eastern arborvitae	2–7	F/PS	W-M-D	M
LARGE TREES (over 50 feet tall)					
Acer rubrum	red maple	2–9	F/PS	M	MPC
Acer saccharum subsp. floridanum	southern sugar maple	6–9	F/PS/S	M	MPC
Betula nigra	river birch	3–9	F/PS	W-M	MPC

Flood-Tolerant Native Trees for Southeastern Landscapes (*continued*)

PLANT NAME *Latin name*	Common name	USDA ZONE	SUNLIGHT	SOIL	SOUTHEAST REGION
Catalpa bignonioides	southern catalpa	5–9	F/PS	M	MPC
Celtis laevigata	southern hackberry	5–10	F/PS	M-D	MPC
Celtis occidentalis	common hackberry	2–9	F/PS/S	M-D	PC
Fraxinus americana	white ash	3–9	F/PS/S	M	MP
Gymnocladus dioica	Kentucky coffee tree	3–8	F/PS	M-D	MP
Liquidambar styraciflua	sweetgum	5–9	F/PS	W-M-D	MPC
Magnolia grandiflora	southern magnolia	6–10	F/PS	M	PC
Magnolia virginiana	sweetbay magnolia	5–9	F/PS	W-M	PC
*Nyssa aquatica**	water tupelo	6–9	F/PS	W-M	C
Nyssa sylvatica	blackgum	3–9	F/PS	W-M-D	MPC
Pinus glabra	spruce pine	7–9	F/PS	W-M-D	MPC
*Pinus taeda**	loblolly pine	6–9	F	W-M-D	MPC
Platanus occidentalis	American sycamore	4–9	F/PS	W-M	MPC
Populus deltoides	eastern cottonwood	2–9	F	W-M	PC
Quercus geminata	sand live oak	7–10	F/PS	W-M-D	C
Quercus laurifolia	laurel oak	7–9	F/PS	W-M	PC
*Quercus michauxii**	swamp chestnut oak	5–9	F/PS	W-M	MPC
*Quercus nigra**	water oak	4–9	F/PS	W-M-D	MPC
*Quercus palustris**	pin oak	4–8	F/PS	W-M-D	PC
*Quercus phellos**	willow oak	5–9	F/PS	W-M-D	PC
Quercus shumardii	Shumard oak	5–9	F/PS	W-M-D	MPC
Quercus texana	Nuttall oak	6–9	F	W-M-D	MPC
Quercus virginiana	live oak	8–10	F/PS	M-D	C
*Taxodium ascendens**	pond cypress	6–10	F/PS	W-M	C
*Taxodium distichum**	bald cypress	4–10	F/PS	W-M	PC
Ulmus alata	winged elm	6–9	F/PS	M-D	MPC

Flood-Tolerant Native Shrubs for Southeastern Landscapes

The following shrubs can withstand short periods of inundation. An asterisk ★
after the Latin name indicates the plant tolerates wet soil year round.

PLANT NAME Latin name	Common name	USDA ZONE	SUNLIGHT	SOIL	SOUTHEAST REGION
Aesculus flava	yellow buckeye	3–8	F/PS	M	MP
Aesculus pavia	red buckeye	4–8	PS	M	PC
Agarista populifolia	coastal leucothoe	7–9	PS/S	M	C
Alnus serrulata	tag alder	4–9	F/PS	W-M	MPC
Aronia arbutifolia	red chokeberry	6–8	F/PS/S	W-M-D	MPC
Aronia melanocarpa	black chokeberry	3–8	F/PS	W-M-D	MP
Baccharis halimifolia★	groundsel bush	5–9	F/PS	W-M-D	MPC
Callicarpa americana	American beautyberry	6–10	F/PS/S	M-D	MPC
Calycanthus floridus	sweetshrub	4–9	F/PS/S	M-D	MPC
Cartrema americana	tea olive	6–9	F/PS/S	M-D	PC
Cephalanthus occidentalis	buttonbush	5–9	F/PS	W-M	MPC
Clethra alnifolia	summersweet	3–9	F/PS/S	W-M	C
Cliftonia monophylla	buckwheat tree	8–9	F/PS	W-M	PC
Comptonia peregrina	sweet fern	2–6	F/PS	M-D	MPC
Crataegus uniflora	dwarf hawthorn	4–9	F/PS	W-M-D	MPC
Dirca palustris	leatherwood	3–9	PS/S	W-M	MP
Euonymus americanus	hearts-a-bustin'	6–9	F/PS	M	MPC
Fothergilla gardenii★	coastal witch alder	5–8	F/PS	W-M	C
Fothergilla latifolia★	witch alder	4–8	F/PS	W-M	MP
Hamamelis virginiana	witch hazel	3–9	F/PS	W-M	MPC
Hibiscus coccineus	scarlet rose mallow	5–9	F/PS	W-M	PC
Hibiscus moscheutos★	rose mallow	5–9	F/PS	W-M	MPC
Hydrangea arborescens	wild hydrangea	3–9	PS	M	MPC
Ilex coriacea	bigleaf gallberry holly	7–9	F/PS	W-M	C

Flood-Tolerant Native Shrubs for Southeastern Landscapes (continued)

PLANT NAME Latin name	Common name	USDA ZONE	SUNLIGHT	SOIL	SOUTHEAST REGION
Ilex glabra*	inkberry	4–11	F/PS	W-M	PC
Ilex verticillata	winterberry holly	3–9	F/PS/S	W-M-D	MPC
Illicium floridanum	anise tree	7–10	PS/S	W-M-D	MPC
Illicium parviflorum	small anise tree	6–9	F/PS/S	W-M-D	MPC
Itea virginica*	Virginia sweet spire	5–9	PS	W-M-D	MPC
Lindera benzoin	spicebush	5–9	PS	W-M-D	MPC
Lyonia lucida*	shining fetterbush	7–9	F/PS/S	W-M	C
Myrica caroliniensis	bayberry	7–9	F/PS	W-M-D	PC
Myrica cerifera*	southern wax myrtle	7–11	F/PS/S	W-M-D	MPC
Myrica pensylvanica	northern bayberry	3–7	F/PS	W-M-D	MPC
Physocarpus opulifolius	ninebark	2–8	F/PS	W-M-D	MP
Rhapidophyllum hystrix	needle palm	7–10	F/PS	W-M-D	C
Rhododendron arborescens*	sweet azalea	4–7	F/PS	W-M	MPC
Rhododendron atlanticum	coastal azalea	6–9	F/PS	W-M-D	C
Rhododendron viscosum*	swamp azalea	4–9	F/PS	W-M	MPC
Sabal minor*	dwarf palmetto	7–10	F/PS	W-M-D	PC
Sabal palmetto	cabbage palm	7–11	F	W-M-D	PC
Sambucus canadensis	elderberry	4–9	F/PS	W-M	MPC
Spiraea tomentosa*	steeplebush spiraea	3–8	F	W-M	MPC
Vaccinium corymbosum*	highbush blueberry	3–8	F/PS	W-M	MPC
Viburnum nudum	smooth withe rod	5–9	F/PS	W-M	MPC
Xanthorhiza simplicissima	yellowroot	3–9	PS	W-M-D	MPC

Flood-Tolerant Native Perennials for Southeastern Landscapes

The following perennials can withstand short periods of inundation. An asterisk *
after the Latin name indicates the plant can grow with constantly wet feet.

PLANT NAME Latin name	Common name	USDA ZONE	SUNLIGHT	SOIL	SOUTHEAST REGION
Amsonia tabernaemontana	eastern bluestar	3–9	F/PS	M	MPC
Asclepias incarnata*	swamp milkweed	3–9	F/PS	W-M	MPC
Baptisia australis	blue false indigo	4–9	F/PS	W-M-D	MPC
Boltonia asteroides	eastern doll's daisy	3–10	F/PS	W-M	MPC
Chelone glabra	white turtlehead	3–8	F/PS	W-M	MPC
Chelone obliqua var. obliqua	purple turtlehead	5–9	F/PS	W-M	MPC
Chrysopsis mariana	Maryland golden aster	4–9	F/PS	M-D	MPC
Conoclinium coelestinum	hardy ageratum	5–9	F/PS	W-M	MPC
Drosera intermedia*	spoonleaf sundew	7–9	F	W-M	MPC
Eupatorium perfoliatum	boneset	3–8	F/PS	W-M	MPC
Eutrochium fistulosum	joe-pye weed	4–8	F/PS	W-M	MPC
Eutrochium maculatum	spotted joe-pye weed	3–8	F/PS	W-M	MPC
Eutrochium purpureum	purple node joe-pye weed	4–8	F/PS	W-M	MPC
Geranium maculatum	wild geranium	3–11	F/PS	M	MP
Helenium autumnale*	autumn sneezeweed	3–8	F/PS	W-M	MPC
Helenium flexuosum*	purple-headed sneezeweed	5–9	F	W-M	MPC
Helianthus angustifolius*	swamp sunflower	5–9	F/PS	W-M	MPC
Hibiscus coccineus	scarlet rose mallow	5–9	F/PS	W-M	PC
Hibiscus grandiflorus*	swamp rose mallow	8–11	F/PS	W-M	C
Hibiscus moscheutos*	rose mallow	5–9	F/PS	W-M	MPC
Iris virginica*	blue flag iris	5–9	F/PS	W-M	MPC
Kosteletzkya pentacarpos*	seashore mallow	6–10	F	W-M	C
Lobelia cardinalis*	cardinal flower	3–9	F/PS	W-M	MPC

Flood-Tolerant Native Perennials for Southeastern Landscapes (continued)

PLANT NAME Latin name	Common name	USDA ZONE	SUNLIGHT	SOIL	SOUTHEAST REGION
Lobelia siphilitica	great blue lobelia	4–9	F/PS	W-M	MP
Marshallia graminifolia	grassleaf Barbara's buttons	7–10	F/PS	W-M	C
Mertensia virginica	Virginia bluebell	3–9	PS/S	W-M	MPC
Mimulus ringens	monkey flower	3–8	F/PS	W-M	MPC
Oenothera fruticosa	sundrops	4–9	F/PS	M-D	MPC
Physostegia purpurea*	savanna obedient plant	8–11	F/PS	W-M	C
Pogonia ophioglossoides*	rose-crested orchid	3–8	F	W-M	MPC
Pycnanthemum virginianum	mountain mint	3–8	F/PS	W-M	MPC
Rudbeckia fulgida	black-eyed Susan	3–9	F	M-D	MPC
Rudbeckia maxima	giant coneflower	4–9	F/PS	M-D	MPC
Sarracenia flava*	yellow pitcher plant	6–9	F	W-M	PC
Saururus cernuus*	lizard's-tail	3–9	F/PS	W	MPC
Senna hebecarpa*	wild senna	4–9	F/PS	W-M	MPC
Silphium perfoliatum	common cup plant	3–9	F/PS	W-M	MP
Solidago caesia	wreath goldenrod	4–8	F/PS	M-D	MPC
Solidago rugosa	rough-stemmed goldenrod	4–8	F/PS	M-D	MPC
Solidago sempervirens*	seaside goldenrod	3–8	F	W-M-D	C
Stokesia laevis	Stokes' aster	5–9	F/PS	W-M	MPC
Symphyotrichum novae-angliae	New England aster	4–8	F/PS	W-M-D	MP
Tradescantia virginiana	Virginia spiderwort	4–9	F/PS/S	W-M	MPC
Vernonanthura nudiflora	sandhills ironweed	7–9	F/PS/S	M-D	C
Vernonia noveboracensis	ironweed	3–9	F	W-M	MPC
Veronicastrum virginicum	Culver's root	3–8	F	W-M	MPC
Viola sororia	common blue violet	3–8	F/PS/S	W-M	MPC

Other Flood-Tolerant Native Plants for Southeastern Landscapes

The following plants can withstand short periods of inundation. An asterisk *
following the Latin name indicates a plant that tolerates wet soil year round.
Please see separate charts for flood-tolerant trees, shrubs, and perennials.

PLANT NAME Latin name	Common name	USDA ZONE	SUNLIGHT	SOIL	SOUTHEAST REGION
FERNS					
Dryopteris intermedia	evergreen wood fern	3–8	PS/S	W-M	MPC
Homalosorus pycnocarpos	glade fern	3–8	PS/S	M	MPC
Onoclea sensibilis	sensitive fern	2–10	F/PS/S	W-M	MPC
Osmundastrum cinnamomeum	cinnamon fern	4–9	F/PS/S	W-M	MPC
Osmunda claytoniana	interrupted fern	3–7	PS/S	W-M-D	MP
Osmunda regalis	royal fern	3–10	F/PS/S	W-M	MPC
Woodwardia virginica	Virginia chain fern	4–10	F/PS/S	W-M-D	MPC
ORNAMENTAL GRASSES					
Andropogon glomeratus	bushy bluestem	7–9	F	W-M	MPC
Aristida stricta	Carolina wire grass	7–10	F/PS	W-M-D	PC
Carex crinita	longhair sedge	3–8	F/PS	W-M	MPC
Carex glaucescens	wax sedge	3–9	F/PS	W-M	PC
Carex lupulina	hop sedge	3–9	PS	W-M	MPC
Carex plantaginea	broadleaf sedge	3–8	PS/S	M	MP
Chasmanthium latifolium	northern sea oats	5–9	F/PS	W-M-D	MPC
Deschampsia cespitosa	tufted hair grass	4–9	F/PS	W-M	MPC
Elymus virginicus	Virginia wild rye	3–8	F/PS	M	MPC
Panicum virgatum	switch grass	3–9	F/PS	W-M-D	MPC
Rhyncospora latifolia	white-topped sedge	7–10	F/PS	W-M	C
Saccharum giganteum	sugarcane plume grass	4–10	F	W-M-D	MPC
Schizachyrium scoparium	little bluestem	3–10	F	W-M-D	C
Scirpus cyperinus*	wool grass bulrush	4–8	F/PS	W-M-D	MPC

Other Flood-Tolerant Native Plants for Southeastern Landscapes (continued)

PLANT NAME Latin name	Common name	USDA ZONE	SUNLIGHT	SOIL	SOUTHEAST REGION
GRASSES USED AS LAWN SUBSTITUTES					
Carex pensylvanica	Pennsylvania sedge	3–8	F/PS/S	M-D	MP
GROUND COVERS					
Rubus hispidus*	swamp dewberry	3–7	PS	W-M	MPC
Rubus trivialis	southern dewberry	4–9	F/PS	W-M-D	MPC
Xanthorhiza simplicissima	yellowroot	3–9	PS	W-M-D	MPC
VINES					
Ampelaster carolinianus	climbing aster	6–10	F/PS	W-M-D	C
Bignonia capreolata	cross vine	5–9	F/PS	M	C
Campsis radicans	trumpet creeper	5–9	F/PS	M	C
Clematis crispa	blue jasmine	6–9	F/PS/S	W-M	MPC
Clematis viorna	northern leatherflower	6–8	F/PS	M	MP
Clematis virginiana	virgin's bower	4–9	F/PS/S	W-M	MPC
Gelsemium rankinii*	swamp jessamine	7–9	F/PS	W-M	C
Gelsemium sempervirens	Carolina jessamine	6–10	F/PS	W-M-D	MPC
Hydrangea barbara	climbing hydrangea	6–9	F/PS/S	W-M	MPC
Lonicera sempervirens	coral honeysuckle	4–9	F/PS	W-M-D	MPC
Parthenocissus quinquefolia	Virginia creeper	4–10	F/PS	W-M-D	MPC
Vitis rotundifolia	muscadine grape	5–9	F/PS	W-M-D	MPC
Wisteria frutescens	American wisteria	5–9	F/PS	M	PC

Salt-Tolerant Native Plants for Southeastern Landscapes

The following plants can stand some salt spray, roadside salt, or temporary bouts of saltwater invasion from a hurricane storm surge. Wash the plants thoroughly with plain water if rainwater has not been sufficient to rinse away the salt accumulation.

PLANT NAME Latin name	Common name	USDA ZONE	SUNLIGHT	SOIL	SOUTHEAST REGION
TREES					
SMALL TREES (up to 30 feet tall)					
Amelanchier laevis	Allegheny serviceberry	4–8	F/PS	M	MPC
Ilex × attenuata 'Fosteri'	Foster's holly	7–9	F/PS	M-D	MPC
Ilex cassine	dahoon holly	7–9	F/PS	W-M	MPC
Ilex vomitoria	yaupon holly	7–9	F/PS/S	W-M-D	PC
Myrica cerifera	southern wax myrtle	7–11	F/PS/S	W-M-D	MPC
Oxydendrum arboreum	sourwood	5–9	F/PS/S	M-D	MPC
MEDIUM TREES (30–50 feet tall)					
Ilex opaca	American holly	5–9	F/PS/S	M-D	MPC
Juniperus virginiana	eastern red cedar	3–9	F/PS	M-D	MPC
Prunus caroliniana	Carolina cherry laurel	7–10	F/PS	M	PC
Zanthoxylum clava-herculis	Hercules' club	7–9	F/PS	M-D	C
LARGE TREES (over 50 feet tall)					
Betula nigra	river birch	3–9	F/PS	W-M	MPC
Celtis laevigata	southern hackberry	5–10	F/PS	M-D	MPC
Fraxinus pennsylvanica	green ash	3–9	F	W-M-D	MPC
Gleditsia triacanthos var. inermis	thornless honey locust	4–9	F	M-D	MPC
Magnolia grandiflora	southern magnolia	6–10	F/PS	M	PC
Magnolia virginiana	sweetbay magnolia	5–9	F/PS	W-M	PC
Nyssa sylvatica	blackgum	3–9	F/PS	W-M-D	MPC
Platanus occidentalis	American sycamore	4–9	F/PS	W-M	MPC

Salt-Tolerant Native Plants for Southeastern Landscapes (continued)

PLANT NAME *Latin name*	*Common name*	USDA ZONE	SUNLIGHT	SOIL	SOUTHEAST REGION
Quercus alba	white oak	3–8	F/PS	M-D	MPC
Quercus geminata	sand live oak	7–10	F/PS	W-M-D	C
Quercus nigra	water oak	4–9	F/PS	W-M-D	MPC
Quercus phellos	willow oak	5–9	F/PS	W-M-D	PC
Quercus virginiana	live oak	8–10	F/PS	M-D	C
Taxodium ascendens	pond cypress	6–10	F/PS	W-M	C
Taxodium distichum	bald cypress	4–10	F/PS	W-M	PC
SHRUBS					
Baccharis halimifolia	groundsel bush	5–9	F/PS	W-M-D	MPC
Callicarpa americana	American beautyberry	6–10	F/PS/S	M-D	MPC
Cartrema americana	tea olive	6–9	F/PS/S	M-D	PC
Ceratiola ericoides	Florida rosemary	8–10	F/PS	M-D	C
Clethra alnifolia	summersweet	3–9	F/PS/S	W-M	C
Hibiscus coccineus	scarlet rose mallow	5–9	F/PS	W-M	PC
Hibiscus moscheutos	rose mallow	5–9	F/PS	W-M	MPC
Hydrangea arborescens	wild hydrangea	3–9	PS	M	MPC
Hypericum tenuifolium	Atlantic St.-John's-wort	8–10	F/PS	M-D	C
Ilex glabra	inkberry	4–11	F/PS	W-M	PC
Ilex verticillata	winterberry holly	3–9	F/PS/S	W-M-D	MPC
Myrica caroliniensis	bayberry	7–9	F/PS	W-M-D	PC
Myrica pensylvanica	northern bayberry	3–7	F/PS	W-M-D	MPC
Opuntia humifusa	eastern prickly-pear cactus	7–10	F/PS	D	MPC
Rhapidophyllum hystrix	needle palm	7–10	F/PS	W-M-D	C
Rhododendron minus	Carolina rhododendron	5–8	PS/S	M-D	MPC
Sabal minor	dwarf palmetto	7–10	F/PS	W-M-D	PC

PLANT NAME Latin name	Common name	USDA ZONE	SUNLIGHT	SOIL	SOUTHEAST REGION
Sabal palmetto	cabbage palm	7–11	F	W-M-D	PC
Serenoa repens	saw palmetto	8–11	F/PS/S	W-M-D	PC
Spiraea tomentosa	steeplebush spiraea	3–8	F	W-M	MPC
Yucca aloifolia	Spanish bayonet	6–11	F/PS	D	PC
Yucca filamentosa	Adam's needle	4–10	F/PS	M-D	MPC
Yucca gloriosa	Spanish dagger	7–11	F/PS	M-D	MPC
Zamia integrifolia	coontie	8–11	F/PS	M-D	C

PERENNIALS AND GRASSES

PLANT NAME Latin name	Common name	USDA ZONE	SUNLIGHT	SOIL	SOUTHEAST REGION
Achillea millefolium	common yarrow	3–9	F	M	MPC
Armeria maritima	sea thrift	4–8	F/PS	M-D	MPC
Asclepias tuberosa	butterfly weed	3–9	F/PS	M-D	MPC
Baptisia australis	blue false indigo	4–9	F/PS	W-M-D	MPC
Chasmanthium latifolium	northern sea oats	5–9	F/PS	W-M-D	MPC
Conradina canescens	beach rosemary	8–10	F	D	C
Coreopsis verticillata	threadleaf coreopsis	3–9	F/PS	M-D	MPC
Deschampsia cespitosa	tufted hair grass	4–9	F/PS	W-M	MPC
Echinacea pallida	pale purple coneflower	3–10	F/PS	M-D	MPC
Echinacea purpurea	purple coneflower	3–8	F/PS	MD	MPC
Eragrostis spectabilis	purple love grass	5–9	F/PS	M-D	MPC
Erythrina herbacea	coral bean	6–11	F/PS	M-D	C
Gaillardia aestivalis	lanceleaf blanketflower	5–9	F	D	MPC
Gaillardia pulchella	beach blanketflower	2–11	F/PS	D	C
Helianthus angustifolius	swamp sunflower	5–9	F/PS	W-M	MPC
Hibiscus coccineus	scarlet rose mallow	5–9	F/PS	W-M	PC
Hibiscus grandiflorus	swamp hibiscus	8–11	F/PS	W-M	C
Hibiscus moscheutos	rose mallow	5–9	F/PS	W-M	MPC

Salt-Tolerant Native Plants for Southeastern Landscapes (continued)

PLANT NAME Latin name	Common name	USDA ZONE	SUNLIGHT	SOIL	SOUTHEAST REGION
Kosteletzkya pentacarpos	seashore mallow	6–10	F	W-M	C
Muhlenbergia capillaris	pink muhly grass	5–9	F	M-D	MPC
Muhlenbergia sericea	purple muhly grass	8–11	F/PS	W-M	C
Panicum amarum	bitter panic grass	2–9	F	M-D	C
Panicum virgatum	switch grass	3–9	F/PS	W-M-D	MPC
Phlox subulata	moss phlox	3–9	F/PS	M-D	MPC
Rudbeckia fulgida	black-eyed Susan	3–9	F	M-D	MPC
Rudbeckia hirta	gloriosa daisy	3–8	F/PS	M-D	MPC
Rudbeckia maxima	giant coneflower	4–9	F/PS	M-D	MPC
Salvia greggii	autumn sage	6–9	F/PS	M-D	MPC
Solidago sempervirens	seaside goldenrod	3–8	F	W-M-D	C
Tridens flavus	purpletop grass	4–9	F/PS	W-D	MPC
Verbena canadensis	rose verbena	6–10	F/PS	M-D	MPC
Verbena stricta	hoary verbena	4–8	F	M-D	MPC

Generalist Native Plants for Southeastern Landscapes

These native plants can be considered "generalists," meaning that, within their designated USDA zone and designated region, they can withstand a wide spectrum of conditions including drought and flood.

PLANT NAME Latin name	Common name	USDA ZONE	SUNLIGHT	SOIL	SOUTHEAST REGION
TREES					
SMALL TREES (up to 30 feet tall)					
Crataegus marshallii	parsley hawthorn	7–9	F/PS/S	W-M-D	PC
Ilex vomitoria	yaupon holly	7–9	F/PS/S	W-M-D	PC
Myrica cerifera	southern wax myrtle	7–11	F/PS/S	W-M-D	MPC
LARGE TREES (over 50 feet tall)					
Fraxinus pennsylvanica	green ash	3–9	F	W-M-D	MPC
Liquidambar styraciflua	sweetgum	5–9	F/PS	W-M-D	MPC
Nyssa sylvatica	blackgum	3–9	F/PS	W-M-D	MPC
Quercus falcata	southern red oak	6–9	F/PS/S	W-M-D	MPC
Quercus geminata	sand live oak	7–10	F/PS	W-M-D	C
Quercus shumardii	Shumard oak	5–9	F/PS	W-M-D	MPC
Quercus texana	Nuttall oak	6–9	F	W-M-D	MPC
Ulmus crassifolia	cedar elm	6–10	F/PS	W-M-D	C
SHRUBS					
Alnus serrulata	tag alder	4–9	F/PS	W-M	MPC
Amorpha fruticosa	indigo bush	3–9	F/PS	W-M	MPC
Aronia arbutifolia	red chokeberry	6–8	F/PS/S	W-M-D	MPC
Aronia melanocarpa	black chokeberry	3–8	F/PS	W-M-D	MP
Baccharis halimifolia	groundsel bush	5–9	F/PS	W-M-D	MPC
Callicarpa americana	American beautyberry	6–10	F/PS/S	M-D	MPC
Calycanthus floridus	sweetshrub	4–9	F/PS/S	M-D	MPC

Generalist Native Plants for Southeastern Landscapes (continued)

PLANT NAME Latin name	Common name	USDA ZONE	SUNLIGHT	SOIL	SOUTHEAST REGION
Cartrema americana	tea olive	6–9	F/PS/S	M-D	PC
Clethra alnifolia	summersweet	3–9	F/PS/S	W-M	C
Comptonia peregrina	sweet fern	2–6	F/PS	M-D	MPC
Crataegus uniflora	dwarf hawthorn	4–9	F/PS	W-M-D	MPC
Euonymus americanus	hearts-a-bustin'	6–9	F/PS	M	MPC
Fothergilla gardenii	coastal witch alder	5–8	F/PS	W-M	C
Fothergilla latifolia	witch alder	4–8	F/PS	W-M	MP
Ilex verticillata	winterberry holly	3–9	F/PS/S	W-M-D	MPC
Illicium floridanum	anise tree	7–10	PS/S	W-M-D	MPC
Illicium parviflorum	small anise tree	6–9	F/PS/S	W-M-D	MPC
Itea virginica	Virginia sweet spire	5–9	F/PS	W-M-D	MPC
Myrica caroliniensis	bayberry	7–9	F/PS	W-M-D	PC
Myrica pensylvanica	northern bayberry	3–7	F/PS	W-M-D	MPC
Physocarpus opulifolius	ninebark	2–8	F/PS	W-M-D	MP
Rhapidophyllum hystrix	needle palm	7–10	F/PS	W-M-D	C
Rhododendron periclymenoides	pinxter bloom azalea	4–9	F/PS	W-M	MPC
Sabal minor	dwarf palmetto	7–10	F/PS	W-M-D	PC
Sabal palmetto	cabbage palm	7–11	F	W-M-D	PC
Serenoa repens	saw palmetto	8–11	F/PS/S	W-M-D	PC
GRASSES					
Aristida stricta	Carolina wire grass	7–10	F/PS	W-M-D	PC
Carex pensylvanica	Pennsylvania sedge	3–8	F/PS/S	M-D	MP
Chasmanthium latifolium	northern sea oats	5–9	F/PS	W-M-D	MPC
Deschampsia cespitosa	tufted hair grass	4–9	F/PS	W-M	MPC

PLANT NAME Latin name	Common name	USDA ZONE	SUNLIGHT	SOIL	SOUTHEAST REGION
Panicum virgatum	switch grass	3–9	F/PS	W-M-D	MPC
Saccharum giganteum	sugarcane plume grass	4–10	F	W-M-D	MPC
Schizachyrium scoparium	little bluestem	3–10	F	W-M-D	MPC
PERENNIALS					
Amsonia tabernaemontana	eastern bluestar	3–9	F/PS	M	MPC
Baptisia australis	blue false indigo	4–9	F/PS	W-M-D	MPC
Chrysopsis mariana	Maryland golden aster	4–9	F/PS	M-D	MPC
Geranium maculatum	wild geranium	3–11	F/PS	M	MP
Helianthus angustifolius	swamp sunflower	5–9	F/PS	W-M	MPC
Oenothera fruticosa	sundrops	4–9	F/PS	M-D	MPC
Phlox carolina	Carolina phlox	3–8	F/PS	W-M-D	MPC
Podophyllum peltatum	mayapple	3–8	PS/S	W-M-D	MP
Polygonatum biflorum	Solomon's seal	3–9	PS/S	W-M-D	MPC
Pycnanthemum tenuifolium	slender mountain mint	4–8	F/PS	W-M-D	MPC
Rudbeckia fulgida	black-eyed Susan	3–9	F	M-D	MPC
Rudbeckia maxima	giant coneflower	4–9	F/PS	M-D	MPC
Salvia lyrata	lyreleaf sage	5–8	F/PS/S	W-M-D	MPC
Solidago caesia	wreath goldenrod	4–8	F/PS	M-D	MPC
Solidago rugosa	rough-stemmed goldenrod	4–8	F/PS	M-D	MPC
Solidago sempervirens	seaside goldenrod	3–8	F	W-M-D	C
Stokesia laevis	Stokes' aster	5–9	F/PS	W-M	MPC
Symphyotrichum novae-angliae	New England aster	4–8	F/PS	W-M-D	MP
Tradescantia ohiensis	smooth spiderwort	4–9	F/PS/S	W-M-D	MPC
Tradescantia virginiana	Virginia spiderwort	4–9	F/PS/S	W-M	MPC
Vernonanthura nudiflora	sandhills ironweed	7–9	F/PS/S	M-D	C
Zizia aurea	golden Alexander	3–8	F/PS	W-M-D	MPC

Generalist Native Plants for Southeastern Landscapes (continued)

PLANT NAME Latin name	Common name	USDA ZONE	SUNLIGHT	SOIL	SOUTHEAST REGION
VINES					
Ampelaster carolinianus	climbing aster	6–9	F/PS	W-M-D	PC
Bignonia capreolata	cross vine	5–9	F/PS	W-M-D	MPC
Campsis radicans	trumpet creeper	4–10	F/PS	W-M-D	MPC
Gelsemium sempervirens	Carolina jessamine	6–10	F/PS	W-M-D	MPC
Lonicera sempervirens	coral honeysuckle	4–9	F/PS	W-M-D	MPC
Parthenocissus quinquefolia	Virginia creeper	4–10	F/PS	W-M-D	MPC
Vitis rotundifolia	muscadine grape	5–9	F/PS	W-M-D	MPC
Wisteria frutescens	American wisteria	5–9	F/PS	W-M-D	PC
FERNS					
Dryopteris intermedia	evergreen wood fern	3–8	PS/S	W-M	MPC
Homalosorus pycnocarpos	glade fern	3–8	PS/S	M	MPC
Osmunda claytoniana	interrupted fern	3–7	PS/S	W-M-D	MP
Woodwardia virginica	Virginia chain fern	4–10	F/PS/S	W-M-D	MPC

Native Evergreen Trees and Shrubs for Southeastern Landscapes

The following list includes broadleaf evergreens as well as fine-needled evergreen conifers.

PLANT NAME Latin name	Common name	USDA ZONE	SUNLIGHT	SOIL	SOUTHEAST REGION
TREES					
SMALL TREES (up to 30 feet tall)					
Ilex × attenuata 'Fosteri'	Foster's holly	7–9	F/PS	M-D	MPC
Ilex × attenuata 'Savannah'	Savannah holly	7–9	F/PS	M-D	MPC
Ilex cassine	dahoon holly	7–9	F/PS	W-M	MPC
Ilex vomitoria	yaupon holly	7–9	F/PS/S	W-M-D	PC
Kalmia latifolia	mountain laurel	4–8	PS	M-D	MP
Myrica cerifera	southern wax myrtle	7–11	F/PS/S	W-M-D	MPC
MEDIUM TREES (30–50 feet tall)					
Abies fraseri	Fraser fir	4–7	F/PS	M	M
Chamaecyparis thyoides	Atlantic white cedar	3–9	F/PS	W-M	C
Gordonia lasianthus	loblolly bay	7–9	F/PS	W-M	C
Ilex opaca	American holly	5–9	F/PS/S	M-D	MPC
Juniperus virginiana	eastern red cedar	3–9	F/PS	M-D	MPC
Persea palustris	swamp bay	7–11	F/PS	W-M-D	C
Pinus virginiana	scrub pine	4–8	F	M-D	MPC
Prunus caroliniana	Carolina cherry laurel	7–10	F/PS	M	PC
Thuja occidentalis	eastern arborvitae	2–7	F/PS	W-M-D	M
LARGE TREES (over 50 feet tall)					
Magnolia grandiflora	southern magnolia	6–10	F/PS	M	PC
Magnolia virginiana	sweetbay magnolia	5–9	F/PS	W-M	PC
Persea borbonia	red bay	7–9	F/PS	W-M	C
Pinus echinata	shortleaf pine	6–9	F/PS	M-D	MPC

Native Evergreen Trees and Shrubs for Southeastern Landscapes (continued)

PLANT NAME Latin name	Common name	USDA ZONE	SUNLIGHT	SOIL	SOUTHEAST REGION
Pinus glabra	spruce pine	7–9	F/PS	W-M-D	MPC
Pinus palustris	longleaf pine	7–9	F	M-D	PC
Pinus strobus	eastern white pine	3–8	F/PS/S	M-D	MP
Pinus taeda	loblolly pine	6–9	F	W-M-D	MPC
Quercus geminata	sand live oak	7–10	F/PS	W-M-D	C
Quercus virginiana	live oak	8–10	F/PS	M-D	C
SHRUBS					
Agarista populifolia	coastal leucothoe	7–9	PS/S	M	C
Cartrema americana	tea olive	6–9	F/PS/S	M-D	PC
Ceratiola ericoides	Florida rosemary	8–10	F/PS	M-D	C
Cliftonia monophylla	buckwheat tree	8–9	F/PS	W-M	PC
Clinopodium coccineum	scarlet wild basil	7–9	F/PS	D	MPC
Hypericum tenuifolium	Atlantic St.-John's-wort	8–10	F/PS	M-D	C
Ilex coriacea	big gallberry	7–9	F/PS	W-M	C
Ilex glabra	inkberry	4–11	F/PS	W-M	PC
Illicium floridanum	anise tree	7–10	PS/S	W-M-D	MPC
Illicium parviflorum	small anise tree	6–9	F/PS/S	W-M-D	MPC
Leucothoe axillaris	coastal dog hobble	5–9	PS	W-M	PC
Lyonia lucida	shining fetterbush	7–9	F/PS/S	W-M	C
Myrica caroliniensis	bayberry	7–9	F/PS	W-M-D	PC
Opuntia humifusa	eastern prickly-pear cactus	7–10	F/PS	D	MPC
Rhapidophyllum hystrix	needle palm	7–10	F/PS	W-M-D	C
Rhododendron catawbiense	catawba rhododendron	4–8	F/PS/S	M-D	MP
Rhododendron maximum	rosebay rhododendron	3–7	F/PS/S	M-D	MP
Rhododendron minus	Carolina rhododendron	5–8	PS/S	M-D	MPC

PLANT NAME Latin name	Common name	USDA ZONE	SUNLIGHT	SOIL	SOUTHEAST REGION
Rhododendron viscosum	swamp azalea	4–9	F/PS	W-M	MPC
Sabal minor	dwarf palmetto	7–10	F/PS	W-M-D	PC
Sabal palmetto	cabbage palm	7–11	F	W-M-D	PC
Serenoa repens	saw palmetto	8–11	F/PS/S	W-M-D	PC
Vaccinium arboreum	huckleberry	7–9	F/PS	M-D	MPC
Viburnum obovatum	small-leaf viburnum	7–10	F/PS	M	PC
Yucca aloifolia	Spanish bayonet	6–11	F/PS	D	PC
Yucca filamentosa	Adam's needle	4–10	F/PS	M-D	MPC
Yucca gloriosa	Spanish dagger	7–11	F/PS	M-D	MPC
Zamia integrifolia	coontie	8–11	F/PS	M-D	C

Native Spring- and Summer-Blooming Trees and Shrubs for Southeastern Landscapes

The following native trees and shrubs bloom in late winter, spring, or summer.

PLANT NAME Latin name	Common name	USDA ZONE	SUNLIGHT	SOIL	SOUTHEAST REGION
TREES					
SMALL TREES (up to 30 feet tall)					
Amelanchier arborea	downy serviceberry	4–9	F/PS	M	MPC
Amelanchier canadensis	eastern serviceberry	3–8	F/PS	M	PC
Amelanchier laevis	smooth serviceberry	4–8	F/PS	M	MPC
Cercis canadensis	eastern redbud	4–9	F/PS	M	MPC
Chionanthus virginicus	fringe tree	3–9	F/PS	M	MPC
Cornus amomum	silky dogwood	4–8	F/PS/S	W-M	MPC
Cornus florida	flowering dogwood	5–9	F/PS	M-D	MPC
Cornus foemina	swamp dogwood	5–9	F/PS	W-M-D	MPC
Cotinus obovatus	American smoke tree	4–8	F/PS	M-D	MPC
Crataegus marshallii	parsley hawthorn	7–9	F/PS/S	W-M-D	PC
Crataegus phaenopyrum	Washington hawthorn	4–8	F/PS	M-D	MPC
Crataegus viridis	green hawthorn	4–8	F	M-D	MPC
Cyrilla racemiflora	titi	5–11	F/PS	W-M	PC
Franklinia alatamaha	franklinia	5–8	F/PS	M	MPC
Kalmia latifolia	mountain laurel	4–8	PS	M-D	MP
Magnolia tripetala	umbrella magnolia	5–8	F/PS	M	MPC
Malus angustifolia	southern crabapple	4–9	F/PS	M	MPC
Oxydendrum arboreum	sourwood	5–9	F/PS/S	M-D	MPC
Pinckneya bracteata	fever tree	7–9	PS	M	PC
Prunus americana	wild plum	4–9	F/PS	M-D	MPC
Sorbus americana	mountain ash	2–6	F/PS	M	MP

PLANT NAME *Latin name*	*Common name*	USDA ZONE	SUNLIGHT	SOIL	SOUTHEAST REGION
Styrax americanus	American silverbell	6–8	F/PS	W-M	MPC
Vaccinium arboreum	huckleberry	7–9	F/PS	M-D	MPC
Viburnum prunifolium	blackhaw viburnum	3–8	F/PS	M-D	MPC
MEDIUM TREES (30–50 feet tall)					
Asimina triloba	pawpaw	5–9	F/PS/S	W-M	MPC
Cladrastis kentukea	yellowwood	4–8	F/PS	M	MP
Crataegus aestivalis	mayhaw	4–8	F/PS	W-M	PC
Gordonia lasianthus	loblolly bay	7–9	F/PS	W-M	C
Halesia carolina	Carolina silverbell	4–8	F/PS	M	MPC
Halesia diptera	two-wing silverbell	5–9	F/PS	W-M	PC
Magnolia macrophylla	bigleaf magnolia	5–8	F/PS	M	MPC
Prunus caroliniana	Carolina cherry laurel	7–10	F/PS	M	PC
Sassafras albidum	sassafras	4–9	F/PS	M-D	MPC
LARGE TREES (over 50 feet tall)					
Aesculus flava	yellow buckeye	3–8	F/PS	M	MP
Catalpa bignonioides	southern catalpa	5–9	F/PS	M	MPC
Cornus alternifolia	pagoda dogwood	3–7	PS/S	W-M	MP
Diospyros virginiana	persimmon	4–9	F/PS	M-D	MPC
Liriodendron tulipifera	tulip tree	4–9	F/PS/S	M-D	MPC
Magnolia grandiflora	southern magnolia	6–10	F/PS	M	PC
Magnolia virginiana	sweetbay magnolia	5–9	F/PS	W-M	PC
Prunus serotina	black cherry	2–8	F	M-D	MPC
Tilia americana	American linden	4–8	F/PS	M-D	MPC
SHRUBS					
Aesculus parviflora	bottlebrush buckeye	4–8	F/PS	M	MPC
Aesculus pavia	red buckeye	4–8	PS	M	PC
Agarista populifolia	fetterbush	7–9	PS/S	M	C

Native Spring- and Summer-Blooming Trees and Shrubs
for Southeastern Landscapes (continued)

PLANT NAME Latin name	Common name	USDA ZONE	SUNLIGHT	SOIL	SOUTHEAST REGION
Amorpha fruticosa	indigo bush	3–9	F/PS	W-M	MPC
Amorpha herbacea	dwarf indigo bush	5–9	F/PS	M	MPC
Aronia arbutifolia	red chokeberry	6–8	F/PS/S	W-M-D	MPC
Aronia melanocarpa	black chokeberry	3–8	F/PS	W-M-D	MP
Asimina parviflora	dwarf pawpaw	7–10	F/PS	M-D	PC
Calycanthus floridus	sweetshrub	4–9	F/PS/S	M-D	MPC
Ceanothus americanus	New Jersey tea	4–8	F/PS	M-D	MPC
Cephalanthus occidentalis	buttonbush	5–9	F/PS	W-M	MPC
Clethra acuminata	mountain pepperbush	6–7	F/PS/S	M	MP
Clethra alnifolia	summersweet	3–9	F/PS/S	W-M	MPC
Cliftonia monophylla	buckwheat tree	8–9	F/PS	W-M	PC
Clinopodium coccineum	scarlet wild basil	7–9	F/PS	D	PC
Crataegus phaenopyrum	Washington hawthorn	4–8	F/PS	M-D	MPC
Diervilla sessilifolia	southern bush honeysuckle	4–8	F/PS	M-D	M
Diospyros virginiana	persimmon	4–9	F/PS	M-D	MPC
Erythrina herbacea	coral bean	6–11	F/PS	M/D	C
Eubotrys racemosa	coastal fetterbush	5–9	PS/S	W-M	PC
Fothergilla gardenii	coastal witch alder	5–8	F/PS	W-M	C
Fothergilla latifolia	witch alder	4–8	F/PS	W-M	MP
Gaylussacia dumosa	dwarf huckleberry	5–9	F/PS	M-D	MPC
Hamamelis virginiana	witch hazel	3–9	F/PS	W-M	MPC
Hibiscus coccineus	scarlet rose mallow	5–9	F/PS	W-M	PC
Hibiscus moscheutos	rose mallow	5–9	F/PS	W-M	MPC
Hydrangea arborescens	wild hydrangea	3–9	PS	M	MPC

PLANT NAME Latin name	Common name	USDA ZONE	SUNLIGHT	SOIL	SOUTHEAST REGION
Hydrangea quercifolia	oakleaf hydrangea	5–9	F/PS	M	MPC
Hydrangea radiata	silverleaf hydrangea	3–9	PS/S	M	MP
Illicium floridanum	anise tree	7–10	PS/S	W-M-D	MPC
Illicium parviflorum	small anise tree	6–9	F/PS/S	W-M-D	MPC
Itea virginica	Virginia sweet spire	5–9	PS	W-M-D	MPC
Leucothoe axillaris	coastal dog hobble	5–9	PS	W-M	PC
Lindera benzoin	spicebush	5–9	PS	W-M-D	MPC
Lyonia lucida	shining fetterbush	7–9	F/PS/S	W-M	C
Philadelphus inodorus	Appalachian mock orange	5–10	F/PS	M-D	MPC
Physocarpus opulifolius	ninebark	2–8	PS/F	W-M-D	MP
Prunus × cistena	purpleleaf sand cherry	2–8	F/PS	M	MPC
Prunus angustifolia	Chickasaw plum	5–8	F	M-D	PC
Rhododendron arborescens	sweet azalea	4–7	F/PS	W-M	MPC
Rhododendron atlanticum	coastal azalea	6–9	F/PS	W-M-D	C
Rhododendron austrinum	Florida flame azalea	7–9	PS	M-D	MPC
Rhododendron calendulaceum	flame azalea	5–7	F/PS/S	M-D	MP
Rhododendron canescens	honeysuckle azalea	5–9	F/PS	W-M-D	MPC
Rhododendron catawbiense	catawba rhododendron	4–8	F/PS/S	M-D	MP
Rhododendron maximum	rosebay rhododendron	3–7	F/PS/S	M-D	MP
Rhododendron minus	Carolina rhododendron	5–8	PS/S	M-D	MPC
Rhododendron periclymenoides	pinxter bloom azalea	4–9	F/PS	W-M	MPC
Rhododendron viscosum	swamp azalea	4–9	F/PS	W-M	MPC
Rhus aromatica	fragrant sumac	3–9	F/PS	M-D	MPC
Rhus copallinum	winged sumac	4–9	F/PS	M-D	MPC
Rubus allegheniensis	Allegheny blackberry	3–8	F/PS	M-D	MPC
Rubus occidentalis	black raspberry	4–8	F/PS	M-D	MPC
Rubus odoratus	purple-flowering raspberry	3–8	F/PS	M	M

Native Spring- and Summer-Blooming Trees and Shrubs
for Southeastern Landscapes (continued)

PLANT NAME Latin name	Common name	USDA ZONE	SUNLIGHT	SOIL	SOUTHEAST REGION
Sambucus canadensis	elderberry	4–9	F/PS	W-M	MPC
Spiraea tomentosa	steeplebush spiraea	3–8	F	W-M	MPC
Stewartia malacodendron	silky camellia	7–9	PS/S	M	MPC
Vaccinium angustifolium	lowbush blueberry	2–8	F/PS/S	M-D	MPC
Vaccinium arboreum	huckleberry	7–9	F/PS	M-D	MPC
Vaccinium corymbosum	highbush blueberry	3–8	F/PS	W-M	MPC
Vaccinium elliottii	Elliott's blueberry	5–9	F/PS	M	PC
Vaccinium pallidum	lowbush blueberry	5–9	F/PS	M-D	MPC
Viburnum dentatum	arrowwood viburnum	3–8	F/PS	M-D	MPC
Viburnum nudum	smooth withe rod	5–9	F/PS	W-M	MPC
Viburnum prunifolium	blackhaw viburnum	3–8	F/PS	M-D	MPC
Xanthorhiza simplicissima	yellowroot	3–9	PS	W-M-D	MPC

Autumn Color from Native Trees for Southeastern Landscapes

The following trees provide autumn interest from richly colored foliage
or from dense berry production.

PLANT Latin name	Common name	USDA ZONE	SUNLIGHT	SOIL	SOUTHEAST REGION
TREES					
SMALL TREES (up to 30 feet tall)					
Acer saccharum subsp. leucoderme	chalk maple	5–9	F/PS/S	M	MP
Amelanchier arborea	downy serviceberry	4–9	F/PS	M	MPC
Amelanchier canadensis	eastern serviceberry	3–8	F/PS	M	PC
Amelanchier laevis	smooth serviceberry	4–8	F/PS	M	MPC
Carpinus caroliniana	American hornbeam	3–9	PS/S	W-D	MPC
Chionanthus virginica	fringe tree	3–9	F/PS	M	MPC
Cornus alternifolia	pagoda dogwood	3–7	PS/S	W-M	MP
Cornus amomum	silky dogwood	4–8	F/PS/S	W-M	MPC
Cornus florida	flowering dogwood	5–9	F/PS	M-D	MPC
Cornus foemina	swamp dogwood	5–9	F/PS	W-M-D	MPC
Cotinus obovatus	American smoke tree	4–8	F/PS	M-D	MPC
Crataegus marshallii	parsley hawthorn	7–9	F/PS/S	W-M-D	PC
Crataegus phaenopyrum	Washington hawthorn	4–8	F/PS	M-D	MPC
Crataegus viridis	green hawthorn	4–8	F	M-D	MPC
Cyrilla racemiflora	titi	5–11	F/PS	W-M	PC
Franklinia alatamaha	franklinia	6–9	F/PS	M	C
Ilex cassine	dahoon holly	7–9	F/PS	W-M	MPC
Ilex decidua	possumhaw	5–9	F/PS	W-M-D	PC
Ilex vomitoria	yaupon holly	7–9	F/PS/S	W-M-D	PC
Oxydendrum arboreum	sourwood	5–9	F/PS/S	M-D	MPC
Prunus americana	American wild plum	3–8	F/PS	M-D	MPC
Sorbus americana	mountain ash	2–6	F/PS	M	MP

Autumn Color from Native Trees for Southeastern Landscapes (*continued*)

PLANT Latin name	Common name	USDA ZONE	SUNLIGHT	SOIL	SOUTHEAST REGION
MEDIUM TREES (30–50 feet tall)					
Acer pensylvanicum	striped maple	3–7	PS/S	M	MP
Asimina triloba	pawpaw	5–9	F/PS/S	W-M	MPC
Cladrastis kentukea	yellowwood	4–8	F/PS	M	MP
Crataegus aestivalis	mayhaw	4–8	F/PS	W-M	PC
Gordonia lasianthus	loblolly bay	7–9	F/PS	W-M	C
Halesia carolina	Carolina silverbell	4–8	F/PS	M	MPC
Halesia diptera	two-wing silverbell	5–9	F/PS	W-M	PC
Ilex opaca	American holly	5–9	F/PS/S	M-D	MPC
Juniperus virginiana	eastern red cedar	3–9	F/PS	M-D	MPC
Ostrya virginiana	American hop hornbeam	3–9	F/PS/S	M-D	MPC
Sassafras albidum	sassafras	4–9	F/PS	M-D	MPC
LARGE TREES (over 50 feet tall)					
Acer rubrum	red maple	2–9	F/PS	M	MPC
Acer saccharum subsp. *floridanum*	southern sugar maple	6–9	F/PS/S	M	MPC
Betula lenta	sweet birch	3–8	F/PS/S	M-D	M
Betula nigra	river birch	3–9	F/PS	W-M	MPC
Carya cordiformis	bitternut hickory	4–9	F	W-M	MPC
Carya glabra	pignut hickory	4–9	F/PS	M-D	MPC
Catalpa bignonioides	southern catalpa	5–9	F/PS	M	MPC
Diospyros virginiana	persimmon	4–9	F/PS	M-D	MPC
Fagus grandifolia	American beech	3–9	F/PS	M	MPC
Fraxinus americana	white ash	3–9	F/PS/S	M	MP
Fraxinus pennsylvanica	green ash	3–9	F	W-M-D	MPC
Gymnocladus dioicus	Kentucky coffee tree	3–8	F/PS	M-D	MP

PLANT Latin name	Common name	USDA ZONE	SUNLIGHT	SOIL	SOUTHEAST REGION
Liquidambar styraciflua	sweetgum	5–9	F/PS	W-M-D	MPC
Liriodendron tulipifera	tulip tree	4–9	F/PS/S	M-D	MPC
Nyssa sylvatica	blackgum	3–9	F/PS	W-M-D	MPC
Prunus serotina	black cherry	2–8	F	M-D	MPC
Quercus alba	white oak	3–8	F/PS	M-D	MPC
Quercus coccinea	scarlet oak	4–9	F/PS	M-D	MPC
Quercus macrocarpa	bur oak	2–8	F/PS	M-D	M
Quercus palustris	pin oak	4–8	F/PS	W-M-D	PC
Quercus rubra	northern red oak	3–8	F/PS	M	MPC
Quercus shumardii	Shumard oak	5–9	F/PS	W-M-D	MPC
Quercus texana	Nuttall oak	6–9	F	W-M-D	MPC
Ulmus crassifolia	cedar elm	6–10	F/PS	W-M-D	C

Autumn Color from Native Shrubs for Southeastern Landscapes

The following shrubs provide autumn interest from richly colored foliage
or from dense berry production.

PLANT NAME Latin nam	Common name	USDA ZONE	SUNLIGHT	SOIL	SOUTHEAST REGION
Aesculus flava	yellow buckeye	3–8	F/PS	M	MP
Aesculus parviflora	bottlebrush buckeye	4–8	F/PS	M	MPC
Agarista populifolia	coastal leucothoe	7–9	PS/S	M	C
Alnus serrulata	tag alder	4–9	F/PS	W-M	MPC
Aronia arbutifolia	red chokeberry	6–8	F/PS/S	W-M-D	MPC
Aronia melanocarpa	black chokeberry	3–8	F/PS	W-M-D	MP
Baccharis halimifolia	groundsel bush	5–9	F/PS	W-M-D	MPC
Callicarpa americana	American beautyberry	6–10	F/PS/S	M-D	MPC
Castanea pumila	Allegheny chinquapin	5–9	F/PS	M-D	MPC
Clethra acuminata	mountain pepperbush	6–7	F/PS/S	M	MP
Clethra alnifolia	summersweet	3–9	F/PS/S	W-M	MPC
Comptonia peregrina	sweet fern	2–6	F/PS	M-D	MPC
Corylus americana	American hazelnut	4–9	F/PS	M-D	MPC
Dirca palustris	leatherwood	3–9	PS/S	W-M	MP
Euonymus americanus	hearts-a-bustin'	6–9	F/PS	M	MPC
Fothergilla gardenii	coastal witch alder	5–8	F/PS	W-M	C
Fothergilla latifolia	witch alder	4–8	F/PS	W-M	MP
Ilex × attenuata 'Fosteri'	Foster's holly	7–9	F/PS	M-D	MPC
Ilex × attenuata 'Savannah'	Savannah holly	7–9	F/PS	M-D	MPC
Ilex verticillata	winterberry holly	3–9	F/PS/S	W-M-D	MPC
Itea virginica	Virginia sweet spire	5–9	PS	W-M-D	MPC
Lindera benzoin	spicebush	5–9	PS	W-M-D	MPC
Rhododendron arborescens	sweet azalea	4–7	F/PS	W-M	MPC

PLANT NAME Latin nam	Common name	USDA ZONE	SUNLIGHT	SOIL	SOUTHEAST REGION
Rhododendron austrinum	Florida flame azalea	7–9	PS	M-D	MPC
Rhus aromatica	fragrant sumac	3–9	F/PS	M-D	MPC
Rhus copallinum	winged sumac	4–9	F/PS	M-D	MPC
Sambucus canadensis	elderberry	4–9	F/PS	W-M	MPC
Stewartia malacodendron	silky camellia	7–9	PS/S	M	MPC
Vaccinium angustifolium	lowbush blueberry	2–8	F/PS/S	M-D	MPC
Vaccinium arboreum	huckleberry	7–9	F/PS	M-D	MPC
Vaccinium corymbosum	highbush blueberry	3–8	F/PS	W-M	MPC
Vaccinium elliottii	Elliott's blueberry	5–9	F/PS	M	PC
Vaccinium pallidum	lowbush blueberry	5–9	F/PS	M-D	MPC
Viburnum dentatum	arrowwood viburnum	3–8	F/PS	M-D	MPC
Viburnum nudum	smooth withe rod	5–9	F/PS	W-M	MPC
Viburnum prunifolium	blackhaw viburnum	3–8	F/PS	M-D	MPC
Xanthorhiza simplicissima	yellowroot	3–9	PS	W-M-D	MPC

Autumn-Blooming Native Perennials for Southeastern Landscapes

The following native perennials bloom in late summer and autumn. In addition to those listed here, there are many native perennials that bloom from early summer into autumn.

PLANT NAME Latin name	Common name	USDA ZONE	SUN-LIGHT	SOIL	SOUTHEAST REGION
Boltonia asteroides	eastern doll's daisy	3–10	F/PS	W-M	MPC
Chrysopsis mariana	Maryland golden aster	4–9	F/PS	M-D	MPC
Conoclinium coelestinum	hardy ageratum	5–9	F/PS	W-M	MPC
Eupatorium perfoliatum	boneset	3–8	F/PS	W-M	MPC
Eurybia divaricata	white wood aster	3–8	PS/S	M-D	MPC
Eurybia macrophylla	bigleaf aster	3–8	PS/S	M-D	MPC
Eutrochium fistulosum	joe-pye weed	4–8	F/PS	W-M	MPC
Eutrochium maculatum	spotted joe-pye weed	3–8	F/PS	W-M	MPC
Eutrochium purpureum	purple node joe-pye weed	4–8	F/PS	W-M	MPC
Gaillardia aestivalis	lanceleaf blanketflower	5–9	F	D	MPC
Helenium autumnale	autumn sneezeweed	3–8	F/PS	W-M	MPC
Helianthus angustifolius	swamp sunflower	5–9	F/PS	W-M	MPC
Hepatica acutiloba	sharp-leaved hepatica	4–8	PS	M	MPC
Heuchera americana	American alumroot	4–9	F/PS/S	M-D	MPC
Hibiscus moscheutos	rose mallow	5–9	F/PS	W-M	MPC
Lobelia cardinalis	cardinal flower	3–9	F/PS	W-M	MPC
Marshallia graminifolia	grassleaf Barbara's buttons	7–10	F/PS	W-M	C
Monarda punctata	spotted bee balm	3–9	F/PS	M-D	MPS
Physostegia purpurea	savanna obedient plant	8–11	F/PS	W-M	C
Physostegia virginiana	obedient plant	2–9	F/PS	W-M	MPC
Silphium perfoliatum	common cup plant	3–9	F/PS	W-M	MP
Solidago caesia	wreath goldenrod	4–8	F/PS	M-D	MPC
Solidago chilensis	licorice goldenrod	4–9	F/PS	M-D	MPC

PLANT NAME Latin name	Common name	USDA ZONE	SUN-LIGHT	SOIL	SOUTHEAST REGION
Solidago rugosa	rough-stemmed goldenrod	4–8	F/PS	M-D	MPC
Solidago sempervirens	seaside goldenrod	3–8	F	W-M-D	C
Solidago speciosa	showy goldenrod	3–8	F	M-D	MPC
Symphyotrichum cordifolium	blue wood aster	3–8	F/PS	M	MPC
Symphyotrichum ericoides	downy aster	3–8	F/PS	M-D	MPC
Symphyotrichum georgianum	Georgia aster	3–9	F	M-D	MPC
Symphyotrichum laeve	smooth blue aster	4–8	F/PS	M-D	MPC
Symphyotrichum lateriflorum	calico aster	4–8	F/PS	M-D	MPC
Symphyotrichum novae-angliae	New England aster	4–8	F/PS	W-M-D	MP
Symphyotrichum oblongifolium	aromatic aster	3–8	F	M-D	MPC
Symphyotrichum patens	late purple aster	4–8	F/PS	M-D	MPC
Symphyotrichum pilosum	frost aster	4–8	F	M-D	MPC
Vernonanthura nudiflora	sandhills ironweed	7–9	F/PS/S	M-D	C
Vernonia noveboracensis	ironweed	3–9	F	W-M	MPC

Native Trees and Shrubs Suitable for Southeast Urban Planting

The following trees and shrubs have been found to withstand urban conditions. However, considerations such as size and need for moisture may restrict how and when they are best used.

PLANT NAME Latin Name	Common Name	USDA ZONE	SUNLIGHT	SOIL	SOUTHEAST REGION
TREES					
SMALL TREES (up to 30 feet tall)					
Acer saccharum subsp. leucoderme	chalk maple	5–9	F/PS/S	M	MP
Aesculus pavia	red buckeye	4–8	PS	M	PC
Amelanchier arborea	downy serviceberry	4–9	F/PS	M	MPC
Amelanchier canadensis	eastern serviceberry	3–8	F/PS	M	PC
Amelanchier laevis	smooth serviceberry	4–8	F/PS	M	MPC
Carpinus caroliniana	American hornbeam	3–9	PS/S	W-M-D	MPC
Cercis canadensis	eastern redbud	4–9	F/PS	M	MPC
Chionanthus virginicus	fringe tree	3–9	F/PS	M	MPC
Cornus alternifolia	pagoda dogwood	3–7	PS/S	W-M	MP
Cornus foemina	swamp dogwood	5–9	F/PS	W-M-D	MPC
Cotinus obovatus	American smoke tree	4–8	F/PS	M-D	MPC
Crataegus marshallii	parsley hawthorn	7–9	F/PS/S	W-M-D	PC
Crataegus phaenopyrum	Washington hawthorn	4–8	F/PS	M-D	MPC
Crataegus viridis	green hawthorn	4–8	F	M-D	MPC
Cyrilla racemiflora	titi	5–11	F/PS	W-M	PC
Ilex × attenuata 'Fosteri'	Foster's holly	7–9	F/PS	M-D	MPC
Ilex cassine	dahoon holly	7–9	F/PS	W-M	MPC
Ilex decidua	possumhaw	5–9	F/PS	W-M-D	PC
Ilex vomitoria	yaupon holly	7–9	F/PS/S	W-M-D	PC
Magnolia tripetala	umbrella magnolia	5–8	F/PS	M	MPC
Malus angustifolia	southern crabapple	4–9	F/PS	M	MPC

PLANT NAME Latin Name	Common Name	USDA ZONE	SUNLIGHT	SOIL	SOUTHEAST REGION
Morus rubra	red mulberry	4–9	F/PS	M-D	MPC
Myrica cerifera	southern wax myrtle	7–11	F/PS/S	W-M-D	MPC
Oxydendrum arboreum	sourwood	5–9	F/PS/S	M-D	MPC
Sorbus americana	mountain ash	2–6	F/PS	M	MP

MEDIUM TREES (30–50 feet tall)

Asimina triloba	pawpaw	5–9	F/PS/S	W-M	MPC
Cladrastis kentuckea	yellowwood	4–8	F/PS	M	MP
Crataegus aestivalis	mayhaw	4–8	F/PS	W-M	PC
Gordonia lasianthus	loblolly bay	7–9	F/PS	W-M	C
Halesia diptera	two-wing silverbell	5–9	F/PS	W-M	PC
Ilex opaca	American holly	5–9	F/PS/S	M-D	MPC
Juniperus virginiana	eastern red cedar	3–9	F/PS	M-D	MPC
Magnolia macrophylla	bigleaf magnolia	5–8	F/PS/S	M	MPC
Ostrya virginiana	American hop hornbeam	3–9	F/PS/S	M-D	MPC
Persea palustris	swamp bay	7–11	F/PS	W-M-D	C
Pinus virginiana	scrub pine	4–8	F	M-D	MPC
Prunus caroliniana	Carolina cherry laurel	7–10	F/PS	M	PC
Sassafras albidum	sassafras	4–9	F/PS	M-D	MPC

LARGE TREES (over 50 feet tall)

Acer rubrum	red maple	2–9	F/PS	M	MPC
Aesculus flava	yellow buckeye	3–8	F/PS	M	MP
Betula nigra	river birch	3–9	F/PS	W-M	MPC
Carya cordiformis	bitternut hickory	4–9	F	W-M	MPC
Carya glabra	pignut hickory	4–9	F/PS	M-D	MPC
Celtis laevigata	sugar hackberry	5–10	F/PS	M-D	MPC
Celtis occidentalis	common hackberry	2–9	F/PS/S	M-D	PC
Diospyros virginiana	persimmon	4–9	F/PS	M-D	MPC

Native Trees and Shrubs Suitable for Southeast Urban Planting (continued)

PLANT NAME Latin Name	Common Name	USDA ZONE	SUNLIGHT	SOIL	SOUTHEAST REGION
Fraxinus americana	white ash	3–9	F/PS/S	M	MP
Fraxinus pennsylvanica	green ash	3–9	F	W-M-D	MPC
Gleditsia triacanthos var. inermis	thornless honey locust	4–9	F	M-D	MPC
Gymnocladus dioicus	Kentucky coffee tree	3–8	F/PS	M-D	MP
Halesia carolina	Carolina silverbell	4–8	F/PS	M	MPC
Liquidambar styraciflua	sweetgum	5–9	F/PS	W-M-D	MPC
Liriodendron tulipifera	tulip tree	4–9	F/PS/S	M-D	MPC
Magnolia grandiflora	southern magnolia	6–10	F/PS	M	PC
Magnolia virginiana	sweetbay magnolia	5–9	F/PS	W-M	PC
Nyssa sylvatica	blackgum	3–9	F/PS	W-M-D	MPC
Persea borbonia	red bay	7–9	F/PS	W-M	C
Pinus glabra	spruce pine	7–9	F/PS	W-M-D	MPC
Platanus occidentalis	American sycamore	4–9	F/PS	W-M	MPC
Prunus serotina	black cherry	2–8	F	M-D	MPC
Quercus alba	white oak	3–8	F/PS	M-D	MPC
Quercus coccinea	scarlet oak	4–9	F/PS	M-D	MPC
Quercus falcata	southern red oak	6–9	F/PS/S	W-M-D	MPC
Quercus lyrata	swamp white oak	5–9	F/PS	W-M	PC
Quercus macrocarpa	bur oak	2–8	F/PS	M-D	M
Quercus michauxii	swamp chestnut oak	5–9	F/PS	W-M	MPC
Quercus montana	chestnut oak	4–8	F/PS	M-D	MPC
Quercus muehlenbergii	chinquapin oak	3–7	F	M-D	MP
Quercus nigra	water oak	4–9	F/PS	W-M-D	MPC
Quercus palustris	pin oak	4–8	F/PS	W-M-D	PC
Quercus phellos	willow oak	5–9	F/PS	W-M-D	PC

PLANT NAME Latin Name	Common Name	USDA ZONE	SUNLIGHT	SOIL	SOUTHEAST REGION
Quercus rubra	northern red oak	3–8	F/PS	M	MPC
Quercus shumardii	Shumard oak	5–9	F/PS	W-M-D	MPC
Quercus stellata	post oak	5–9	F	M-D	MP
Quercus texana	Nuttall oak	6–9	F	W-M-D	MPC
Quercus virginiana	live oak	8–10	F/PS	M-D	C
Taxodium ascendens	pond cypress	6–10	F/PS	W-M	C
Taxodium distichum	bald cypress	4–10	F/PS	W-M	PC
Tilia americana	American linden	4–8	F/PS	M-D	MPC
Ulmus alata	winged elm	6–9	F/PS	M-D	MPC
Ulmus crassifolia	cedar elm	6–10	F/PS	W-M-D	PC
SHRUBS					
Ceanothus americanus	New Jersey tea	4–8	F/PS	M-D	MPC
Prunus × cistena	purpleleaf sand cherry	2–8	F/PS	M	MPC
Rhus copallinum	winged sumac	4–9	F/PS	M-D	MPC

Recommended Native Ferns for Southeastern Landscapes

The following list includes excellent native ferns for the Southeast.
An asterisk * next to the Latin name indicates that the fern is evergreen.

PLANT NAME Latin name	Common name	USDA ZONE	SUNLIGHT	SOIL	SOUTHEAST REGION
Adiantum capillus-veneris	southern maidenhair fern	6–9	PS/S	M	C
Adiantum hispidulum	northern maidenhair fern	3–8	PS/S	M	MPC
Asplenium platyneuron*	ebony spleenwort	3–9	PS/S	M-D	MPC
Athyrium asplenioides	southern lady fern	5–9	PS/S	M-D	MPC
Botrychium virginianum	rattlesnake fern	4–9	PS/S	M-D	MPC
Deparia acrostichoides	silvery glade fern	4–9	F/PS/S	M	MPC
Dryopteris × australis	Dixie wood fern	5–9	PS/S	W-M-D	C
Dryopteris cristata*	crested wood fern	3–7	PS/S	W-M	MP
Dryopteris intermedia*	evergreen wood fern	3–8	PS/S	W-M	MPC
Dryopteris marginalis*	marginal wood fern	4–9	PS/S	M	MPC
Hemionitis lanosa	woolly fern	5–8	F/PS	M-D	MPC
Homalosorus pycnocarpos	glade fern	3–8	PS/S	M	MPC
Onoclea sensibilis	sensitive fern	2–10	F/PS/S	W-M	MPC
Osmundastrum cinnamomeum	cinnamon fern	4–9	F/PS/S	W-M	MPC
Osmunda claytoniana	interrupted fern	3–7	PS/S	W-M-D	MP
Osmunda regalis	royal fern	3–10	F/PS/S	W-M	MPC
Polystichum acrostichoides*	Christmas fern	3–9	PS/S	M-D	MPC
Thelypteris normalis	southern shield fern	7–10	PS/S	M-D	MPC
Thelypteris noveboracensis	New York fern	3–8	PS/S	M-D	MPC
Woodwardia areolata*	netted chain fern	3–9	PS/S	W-M	MPC
Woodwardia virginica	Virginia chain fern	4–10	F/PS/S	W-M-D	MPC

Recommended Native Grasses for Southeastern Landscapes

The following list includes ornamental grasses, lawn grasses,
and lawn grass substitutes.

PLANT NAME Latin Name	Common Name	USDA ZONE	SUNLIGHT	SOIL	SOUTHEAST REGION
ORNAMENTAL GRASSES					
Acorus calamus	sweet flag sedge	4–10	F/PS	W-M	MPC
Andropogon gerardii	big bluestem	4–9	F	M-D	MPC
Andropogon glomeratus	bushy bluestem	7–9	F	W-M	MPC
Andropogon ternarius	splitbeard bluestem	5–10	F/PS	M-D	MPC
Andropogon virginicus	broom sedge	3–9	F/PS	M-D	MPC
Aristida stricta	Carolina wire grass	7–10	F/PS	W-M-D	PC
Carex crinita	fringed sedge	3–8	F/PS	W-M	MPC
Carex flaccosperma	blue wood sedge	5–9	PS/S	M-D	MPC
Carex fraseriana	Fraser's sedge	5–7	PS/S	M	M
Carex glaucescens	wax sedge	3–9	PS/S	W-M	MPC
Carex lupulina	hop sedge	3–9	PS/S	W-M	MPC
Carex plantaginea	seersucker sedge	3–8	PS/S	M	MP
Chasmanthium latifolium	northern sea oats	5–9	F/PS	W-M-D	MPC
Deschampsia cespitosa	tufted hair grass	4–9	F/PS	W-M	MPC
Elymus hystrix	bottlebrush grass	5–8	PS/S	M-D	MP
Elymus virginicus	Virginia wild rye	3–8	F/PS	M	MPC
Eragrostis spectabilis	purple love grass	5–9	F/PS	M-D	MPC
Muhlenbergia capillaris	pink muhly grass	5–9	F	M-D	MPC
Muhlenbergia sericea	purple muhly grass	8–11	F/PS	W-M	C
Panicum amarum	bitter panic grass	2–9	F	M-D	C
Panicum virgatum	switch grass	3–9	F/PS	W-M-D	MPC
Rhyncospora latifolia	white-topped sedge	7–10	F/PS	W-M	C

Recommended Native Grasses for Southeastern Landscapes (*continued*)

PLANT NAME *Latin Name*	*Common Name*	USDA ZONE	SUNLIGHT	SOIL	SOUTHEAST REGION
Saccharum giganteum	sugarcane plume grass	4–10	F	W-M-D	MPC
Schizachyrium scoparium	little bluestem	3–10	F	W-M-D	MPC
Sisyrinchium angustifolium	narrow-leaved blue-eyed grass	4–9	F/PS	M-D	MPC
Sisyrinchium mucronatum	needle-tip blue-eyed grass	3–8	F/PS	M-D	MPC
Sorghastrum nutans	yellow Indian grass	4–9	F	M-D	MPC
Tridens flavus	purpletop grass	4–9	F/PS	W-D	MPC
LAWN GRASSES AND LAWN GRASS SUBSTITUTES					
Axonopus compressus	blanket grass	7–10	F/PS	W-M	MPC
Axonopus fissifolius	common carpet grass	7–10	F/PS	M	PC
Calyptocarpus vialis	straggler daisy	8–10	F/PS/S	M-D	MPC
Carex laxiculmis	glaucous wood sedge	4–9	PS/S	W-M	MP
Carex pensylvanica	Pennsylvania sedge	3–8	F/PS/S	M-D	MP
Erigeron pulchellus	robin's plantain	3–8	F/PS	M	MPC
Muhlenbergia schreberi	nimble will	6–11	F/PS	M-D	MPC
Stenotaphrum secundatum	St. Augustine grass	8–10	F	M-D	C

Recommended Native Groundcovers for Southeastern Landscapes

The following list includes native groundcovers for a variety of growing conditions.

PLANT NAME *Latin name*	*Common name*	USDA ZONE	SUNLIGHT	SOIL	SOUTHEAST REGION
Asarum arifolium	heartleaf ginger	5–8	F/PS/S	M-D	MPC
Asarum canadense	wild ginger	4–6	PS/S	W-M	MPC
Berberis repens	creeping mahonia	4–9	F/PS/S	M-D	MPC
Calyptocarpus vialis	straggler daisy	8–10	F/PS/S	M-D	MPC
Chrysogonum virginianum	green-and-gold	6–8	PS/S	M	MPC
Dyschoriste oblongifolia	oblongleaf twinflower	8–11	F/PS	M-D	PC
Erigeron pulchellus	robin's plantain	3–8	F/PS	M	MPC
Fragaria virginiana	wild strawberry	2–9	F/PS	M-D	MP
Gaultheria procumbens	American wintergreen	3–7	PS/S	M-D	MPC
Heuchera americana	American alumroot	4–9	F/PS/S	M-D	MPC
Hexastylis shuttleworthii	little brown jug	5–8	PS	M	MP
Juniperus communis var. depressa	ground juniper	2–6	F/PS/S	M-W	MPC
Mitchella repens	partridgeberry	3–8	F/PS/S	M-D	MPC
Onoclea sensibilis	sensitive fern	2–10	F/PS/S	W-M	MPC
Pachysandra procumbens	Allegheny spurge	5–9	PS/S	M	MPC
Phlox nivalis	trailing phlox	6–8	F/PS	M-D	MPC
Polystichum acrostichoides	Christmas fern	3–9	PS/S	M-D	MPC
Rubus flagellaris	northern dewberry	3–8	F/PS/S	M-D	MPC
Rubus hispidus	swamp dewberry	3–7	PS	W-M	MPC
Rubus trivialis	southern dewberry	4–9	F/PS	W-M-D	MPC
Sedum ternatum	mountain stonecrop	4–9	PS/S	M-D	MP
Tiarella cordifolia	heartleaf foamflower	3–8	PS/S	M	MPC
Vaccinium crassifolium	creeping blueberry	6–9	F/PS	M-D	PC
Veronica repens	creeping speedwell	2–9	F/PS	M	MPC
Woodwardia areolata	netted chain fern	3–9	PS/S	W-M	MPC
Xanthorhiza simplicissima	yellowroot	3–9	PS	W-M-D	MPC
Zamia integrifolia	coontie	8–11	F/PS	M-D	C

Recommended Native Perennials for Southeastern Landscapes

There are many hundreds of wonderful perennial plants native to the Southeast.
This list represents a selection of 150 of the best, but is not at all meant to be exclusive.
See chapter 12 for resources in your state, which can suggest some native perennials
not listed here. Note: Almost all of these plants have multiple common names;
therefore you may know the plant by another name.

PLANT NAME Latin name	Common name	USDA ZONE	SUNLIGHT	SOIL	SOUTHEAST REGION
Achillea millefolium	common yarrow	3–9	F	M	MPC
Actaea pachypoda	doll's eyes	3–8	PS/S	M	MP
Actaea racemosa	black cohosh	4–8	PS/S	M	MPC
Agave virginica	false aloe	6–9	F/PS	D	MPC
Allium cernuum	nodding onion	4–8	F/PS	M-D	MP
Amsonia tabernaemontana	eastern bluestar	3–9	F/PS	M	MPC
Anemonoides quinquefolia	wood anemone	3–8	PS/S	M	MPC
Aquilegia canadensis	eastern columbine	3–8	F/PS	M-D	MPC
Arisaema triphyllum	jack-in-the-pulpit	4–9	PS/S	W-M	MPC
Armeria maritima	sea thrift	4–8	F/PS	M-D	MPC
Artemisia ludoviciana	white sage	4–10	F	W-M-D	MPC
Asclepias incarnata	swamp milkweed	3–9	F/PS	W-M	MPC
Asclepias purpurascens	purple milkweed	3–8	F/PS	M-D	MPC
Asclepias tuberosa	butterfly weed	3–9	F/PS	M-D	MPC
Baptisia alba	false indigo	5–8	F/PS	M-D	PC
Baptisia australis	blue false indigo	4–9	F/PS	W-M-D	MPC
Boltonia asteroides	eastern doll's daisy	3–10	F/PS	W-M	MPC
Camassia scilloides	wild hyacinth	4–8	F/PS	M	PC
Chelone glabra	white turtlehead	3–8	F/PS	W-M	MPC
Chelone lyonii	pink turtlehead	3–8	F/PS	W-M	MP
Chrysopsis mariana	Maryland golden aster	4–9	F/PS	M-D	MPC

PLANT NAME *Latin name*	Common name	USDA ZONE	SUNLIGHT	SOIL	SOUTHEAST REGION
Claytonia virginica	spring beauty	3–8	PS	M	MPC
Clintonia umbellulata	Clinton's lily	4–7	S	M-D	M
Conoclinium coelestinum	hardy ageratum	5–9	F/PS	W-M	MPC
Conradina canescens	beach rosemary	8–10	F	D	C
Coreopsis auriculata	mouse-ear coreopsis	4–9	F/PS	M-D	MPC
Coreopsis grandiflora	large-flowered coreopsis	4–9	F/PS	D	MPC
Coreopsis lanceolata	lanceleaf coreopsis	4–9	F/PS	M-D	MPC
Coreopsis major	woodland coreopsis	5–9	F/PS	M-D	MPC
Coreopsis rosea	pink coreopsis	3–8	F	M	MPC
Coreopsis tripteris	tall coreopsis	3–8	F	M-D	MPC
Coreopsis verticillata	threadleaf coreopsis	3–9	F/PS	M-D	MPC
Dicentra cucullaria	Dutchman's-breeches	3–7	PS	M	MPC
Dicentra eximia	bleeding heart	4–8	PS	M	MP
Drosera intermedia	spoonleaf sundew	7–9	F	W-M	MPC
Dyschoriste oblongifolia	oblongleaf twinflower	7–10	F/PS	M-D	PC
Echinacea pallida	pale purple coneflower	3–10	F/PS	M-D	MPC
Echinacea purpurea	purple coneflower	3–8	F/PS	MD	MPC
Eryngium yuccifolium	rattlesnake master	5–9	F	D	MPC
Erythrina herbacea	coral bean	6–11	F/PS	M-D	C
Erythronium americanum	trout lily	3–8	PS/S	M	MPC
Eupatorium perfoliatum	boneset	3–8	F/PS	W-M	MPC
Eupatorium rugosum	white snakeroot	3–9	F/PS/S	M-D	MPC
Eurybia divaricata	white wood aster	3–8	PS/S	M-D	MPC
Eurybia macrophylla	bigleaf aster	3–8	PS/S	M-D	MPC
Eutrochium fistulosum	joe-pye weed	4–8	F/PS	W-M	MPC
Eutrochium maculatum	spotted joe-pye weed	3–8	F/PS	W-M	MPC
Gaillardia pulchella	beach blanketflower	2–11	F/PS	D	C

Recommended Native Perennials for Southeastern Landscapes (*continued*)

PLANT NAME Latin name	Common name	USDA ZONE	SUNLIGHT	SOIL	SOUTHEAST REGION
Geranium maculatum	wild geranium	3–11	F/PS	M	MP
Geum canadense	white avens	4–8	F/PS/S	W-M-D	MP
Helenium autumnale	autumn sneezeweed	3–8	F/PS	W-M	MPC
Helianthus angustifolius	swamp sunflower	5–9	F/PS	W-M	MPC
Helianthus divaricatus	woodland sunflower	3–9	PS	M-D	MPC
Heliopsis helianthoides	false sunflower	3–9	F/PS	M-D	MPC
Hepatica americana	round-lobed hepatica	3–8	PS	M	MPC
Heuchera americana	American alumroot	4–9	F/PS/S	M-D	MPC
Hibiscus coccineus	scarlet rose mallow	5–9	F/PS	W-M	PC
Hibiscus grandiflorus	swamp rose mallow	8–11	F/PS	W-M	C
Hibiscus moscheutos	rose mallow	5–9	F/PS	W-M	MPC
Hymenocallis occidentalis var. occidentalis	woodland spider lily	5–8	F/PS	W-M	MPC
Hypericum prolificum	shrubby St.-John's-wort	4–8	F/PS	M-D	MPC
Impatiens capensis	jewelweed	2–11	PS/S	W-M	MPC
Iris cristata	dwarf crested iris	3–9	PS	M-D	MPC
Iris fulva	copper iris	5–9	F/PS	W-M	MPC
Iris verna	dwarf iris	6–8	F/PS	M	MPC
Iris virginica	blue flag iris	5–9	F/PS	W-M	MPC
Kosteletzkya pentacarpos	seashore mallow	6–10	F	W-M	C
Liatris spicata	blazing star	3–8	F/PS	W-M-D	MPC
Lilium canadense	Canada lily	3–8	F	W-M	MPC
Lilium michauxii	Carolina lily	6–9	PS	M	MPC
Lilium superbum	Turk's-cap lily	5–8	F/PS	W-M	MPC
Lobelia cardinalis	cardinal flower	3–9	F/PS	W-M	MPC
Lobelia siphilitica	great blue lobelia	4–9	F/PS	W-M	MP

Plant name *Latin name*	Common name	USDA ZONE	SUNLIGHT	SOIL	SOUTHEAST REGION
Lupinus perennis	sundial lupine	4–8	F/PS	M-D	PC
Lysimachia ciliata	fringed loosestrife	4–9	F/PS	W-M-D	MPC
Maianthemum racemosum	false Solomon's seal	4–8	PS	M	MPC
Marshallia graminifolia	grassleaf Barbara's buttons	7–10	F/PS	W-M	C
Mertensia virginica	Virginia bluebell	3–9	PS/S	W-M	MPC
Mimulus ringens	monkey flower	3–8	F/PS	W-M	MPC
Monarda didyma	scarlet bee balm	3–8	F/PS	W-M	MPC
Monarda fistulosa	wild bergamot	3–9	F/PS	M-D	MP
Monarda punctata	spotted bee balm	3–9	F/PS	M-D	MPC
Oenothera fruticosa	sundrops	4–9	F/PS	M-D	MPC
Oenothera lindheimeri	gaura	5–9	F/PS	D	MPC
Oenothera speciosa	pink evening primrose	5–8	F/PS	M-D	MPC
Opuntia humifusa	eastern prickly-pear cactus	4–9	F	D	MPC
Packera aurea	groundsel	4–9	F/PS/S	W-M	MPC
Penstemon australis	southern beardtongue	5–9	F/PS	M-D	PC
Penstemon digitalis	white beardtongue	3–8	F	M-D	MP
Penstemon laevigatus	eastern smooth beardtongue	6–8	F/PS/S	M-D	MPC
Phlox carolina	Carolina phlox	3–8	F/PS	W-M-D	MPC
Phlox divaricata	woodland phlox	3–8	PS/S	M	MPC
Phlox nivalis	trailing phlox	6–9	F/PS	M-D	MPC
Phlox paniculata	garden phlox	4–8	F/PS	M	MPC
Phlox stolonifera	creeping phlox	5–8	F/PS	M-D	MPC
Phlox subulata	moss phlox	3–9	F/PS	M-D	MPC
Physostegia virginiana	obedient plant	2–9	F/PS	W-M	MPC
Podophyllum peltatum	mayapple	3–8	PS/S	W-M-D	MP
Pogonia ophioglossoides	rose-crested orchid	3–8	F	W-M	MPC
Polemonium reptans	Jacob's ladder	2–8	F/PS	M	M
Polygonatum biflorum	Solomon's seal	3–9	PS/S	W-M-D	MPC

Recommended Native Perennials for Southeastern Landscapes (continued)

PLANT NAME Latin name	Common name	USDA ZONE	SUNLIGHT	SOIL	SOUTHEAST REGION
Primula meadia	shooting star	4–8	PS	M	MP
Prunella vulgaris	self-heal	3–9	F/PS	M	MPC
Pycnanthemum incanum	silverleaf mountain mint	4–8	F/PS	M-D	MP
Pycnanthemum tenuifolium	slender mountain mint	4–8	F/PS	W-M-D	MPC
Pycnanthemum virginianum	mountain mint	3–8	F/PS	W-M	MPC
Rudbeckia fulgida	black-eyed Susan	3–9	F	M-D	MPC
Rudbeckia hirta	gloriosa daisy	3–8	F/PS	M-D	MPC
Rudbeckia laciniata	green-headed coneflower	3–9	F/PS	M	MPC
Rudbeckia maxima	giant coneflower	4–9	F/PS	M-D	MPC
Ruellia caroliniensis	Carolina wild petunia	6–11	PS	M-D	MPC
Salvia coccinea	scarlet sage	8–10	F/PS	M-D	PC
Salvia greggii	autumn sage	6–9	F/PS	M-D	MPC
Salvia lyrata	lyreleaf sage	5–8	F/PS/S	W-M-D	MPC
Sanguinaria canadensis	bloodroot	3–8	PS/S	M	MPC
Sarracenia flava	yellow pitcher plant	6–9	F	W-M	PC
Scutellaria incana	downy skullcap	5–8	PS	M-D	MPC
Sedum ternatum	mountain stonecrop	4–9	PS/S	M-D	MP
Silene regia	royal catchfly	4–9	F/PS	M-D	MPC
Silene virginica	fire pink	4–8	F/PS	M-D	MPC
Silphium perfoliatum	common cup plant	3–9	F/PS	W-M	MP
Solidago caesia	wreath goldenrod	4–8	F/PS	M-D	MPC
Solidago chilensis	licorice goldenrod	4–9	F/PS	M-D	MPC
Solidago rugosa	rough-stemmed goldenrod	4–8	F/PS	M-D	MPC
Solidago sempervirens	seaside goldenrod	3–8	F	W-M-D	C
Solidago speciosa	showy goldenrod	3–8	F	M-D	MPC
Spigelia marilandica	Indian pink	5–9	PS	M	MPC

PLANT NAME Latin name	Common name	USDA ZONE	SUNLIGHT	SOIL	SOUTHEAST REGION
Stokesia laevis	Stokes' aster	5–9	F/PS	W-M	MPC
Stylophorum diphyllum	celandine poppy	4–8	PS/S	W-M	MP
Symphyotrichum cordifolium	blue wood aster	3–8	F/PS	M	MPC
Symphyotrichum ericoides	downy aster	3–8	F/PS	M-D	MPC
Symphyotrichum georgianum	Georgia aster	3–9	F	M-D	MPC
Symphyotrichum laeve	smooth blue aster	4–8	F/PS	M-D	MPC
Symphyotrichum lateriflorum	calico aster	4–8	F/PS	M-D	MPC
Symphyotrichum novae-angliae	New England aster	4–8	F/PS	W-M-D	MP
Thermopsis villosa	Carolina lupine	3–10	F/PS	M	MP
Tiarella cordifolia	heartleaf foamflower	3–8	PS/S	M	MPC
Tradescantia ohiensis	smooth spiderwort	4–9	F/PS/S	W-M-D	MPC
Tradescantia virginiana	Virginia spiderwort	4–9	F/PS/S	W-M	MPC
Trillium catesbaei	Catesby's trillium	4–9	PS/S	M	MP
Trillium cernuum	nodding trillium	5–8	PS/S	M	MP
Trillium cuneatum	sweet Betsy	5–8	PS/S	M	MP
Trillium lancifolium	lanceleaf trillium	5–9	PS/S	M	MP
Trillium maculatum	mottled trillium	5–9	PS/S	M	MP
Uvularia grandiflora	bellwort	4–9	PS/S	M	MP
Verbena canadensis	rose verbena	6–10	F/PS	M-D	MPC
Verbena stricta	hoary verbena	4–8	F	M-D	MPC
Vernonia gigantea	giant ironweed	5–8	F/PS	W-M	MPC
Vernonia noveboracensis	ironweed	3–9	F	W-M	MPC
Veronicastrum virginicum	Culver's root	3–8	F	W-M	MPC
Viola canadensis	Canada violet	3–8	PS	M	MP
Viola pedata	bird's-foot violet	4–8	F/PS	M	MPC
Viola sororia	common blue violet	3–8	F/PS/S	W-M	MPC
Yucca filamentosa	Adam's needle	4–10	F?PS	M-D	MPCC
Zephyranthes atamasco	rain lily	7–10	F/PS/S	W-M	MPC
Zizia aurea	golden Alexander	3–8	F/PS	W-M-D	MPC

Recommended Native Vines for Southeastern Landscapes

Native vines tend to be vigorous. Plant them where you can keep them under control.

PLANT NAME Latin name	Common name	USDA ZONE	SUNLIGHT	SOIL	SOUTHEAST REGION
Ampelaster carolinianus	climbing aster	6–9	F/PS	W-M-D	PC
Aristolochia macrophylla	Dutchman's-pipe vine	4–8	PS	M-D	M
Aristolochia tomentosa	woolly Dutchman's-pipe vine	5–8	F/PS	W-M-D	MPC
Bignonia capreolata	cross vine	5–9	F/PS	W-M-D	MPC
Campsis radicans	trumpet creeper	4–10	F/PS	W-M-D	MPC
Clematis crispa	blue jasmine	6–9	F/PS/S	W-M	MPC
Clematis viorna	northern leatherflower	4–9	F/PS	W-M	MPC
Clematis virginiana	virgin's bower	4–9	F/PS/S	W-M	MPC
Gelsemium rankinii	swamp jessamine	7–9	F/PS	W-M	C
Gelsemium sempervirens	Carolina jessamine	6–10	F/PS	W-M-D	MPC
Hydrangea barbara	climbing hydrangea	6–9	F/PS/S	W-M	MPC
Lonicera sempervirens	coral honeysuckle	4–9	F/PS	W-M-D	MPC
Parthenocissus quinquefolia	Virginia creeper	4–10	F/PS	W-M-D	MPC
Passiflora incarnata	passionflower vine	5–9	F/PS	M-D	MPC
Vitis rotundifolia	muscadine grape	5–9	F/PS	W-M-D	MPC
Wisteria frutescens	American wisteria	5–9	F/PS	W-M-D	PC

Suggested Native Substitutes for Popular Nonnative (Exotic) Plants

These are some of the most commonly used landscape plants, with suggested native alternatives. The (inv.) following the common name indicates that this plant is a known invasive in one or more southeastern states. Growing areas for natives are marked M (Mountains), P (Piedmont), and C (Coastal Plain). For details on the native plants' cultural needs, height, shape, flower color, and more, consult the North Carolina Extension Gardener Plant Toolbox (https://plants.ces.ncsu.edu).

POPULAR SMALL-TO-MEDIUM EVERGREEN AND SEMIEVERGREEN EXOTIC SHRUBS

Berberis thunbergii	Japanese barberry (inv.)
Buxus microphylla	Korean boxwood
Distylium spp.	distylium
Euonymus japonicus microphyllus	dwarf euonymus
Ilex cornuta	dwarf Chinese holly
Ilex crenata	Japanese holly
Loropetalum chinense	dwarf loropetalum
Podocarpus macrophyllus	dwarf podocarpus
Rhaphiolepis indica	dwarf Indian hawthorn

SUGGESTED NATIVE SUBSTITUTES

Ceratiola ericoides	Florida rosemary (C)
Ilex glabra	inkberry (PC)
Lyonia lucida	shining fetterbush (C)
Rhododendron minus	Carolina rhododendron (MPC)
Viburnum obovatum	littleleaf viburnum (PC)

POPULAR MEDIUM-TO-LARGE EVERGREEN AND SEMIEVERGREEN EXOTIC SHRUBS

Elaeagnus angustifolia	Russian olive (inv.)
Elaeagnus umbellata	autumn olive (inv.)
Ilex aquifolium	European holly
Ilex cornuta	Chinese holly (inv.)
Ligustrum japonicum	Japanese privet (inv.)
Ligustrum sinense	Chinese privet (inv.)
Nandina domestica	nandina (inv.)
Pieris japonica	Japanese andromeda

Suggested Native Substitutes for Popular Nonnative (Exotic) Plants (continued)

Pittosporum spp.	pittosporum
Podocarpus macrophyllus	Chinese podocarpus
Rhamnus cathartica	buckthorn (inv.)
Rhaphiolepis indica	Indian hawthorn
Taxus cuspidata	Japanese yew

SUGGESTED NATIVE SUBSTITUTES

Agarista populifolia	coastal fetterbush (C)
Calycanthus floridus	sweetshrub (MPC)
Castanea pumila	Allegheny chinquapin (MPC)
Ilex coriacea	bigleaf gallberry (C)
Illicium floridanum	Florida anise tree (MPC)
Illicium parviflorum	small anise tree (MPC)
Myrica caroliniensis	bayberry (PC)
Myrica cerifera	southern wax myrtle (MPC)
Myrica pensylvanica	northern bayberry (MPC)

POPULAR SPRING-BLOOMING EXOTIC TREES

Ailanthus altissima	tree of heaven (inv.)
Albizia julibrissin	mimosa (inv.)
Magnolia × soulangeana	tulip magnolia
Magnolia stellata	star magnolia
Melia azedarach	chinaberry (inv.)
Paulownia tomentosa	princess tree (inv.)
Prunus 'Okame'	Okame cherry
Prunus × yedoensis	Yoshino cherry
Prunus serrulata 'Kanzan'	Kwanzan cherry
Pyrus calleryana	Bradford pear (inv.)
Triadica sebifera	popcorn tree (inv.)

Amelanchier arborea	downy serviceberry (MPC)
Amelanchier canadensis	eastern serviceberry (PC)
Amelanchier laevis	Allegheny serviceberry (MPC)
Cercis canadensis	redbud (MPC)
Cornus alternifolia	pagoda dogwood (MP)
Cornus florida	flowering dogwood (MPC)
Crataegus aestivalis	mayhaw (PC)
Crataegus marshallii	parsley hawthorn (PC)
Crataegus phaenopyrum	Washington hawthorn (MPC)
Diospyros virginiana	persimmon (MPC)
Franklinia alatamaha	franklinia (MPC)
Halesia carolina	Carolina silverbell (MPC)
Halesia diptera	two-winged silverbell (PC)
Magnolia tripetala	umbrella tree (MPC)
Magnolia virginiana	sweetbay magnolia (PC)
Malus angustifolia	southern crabapple (MPC)
Pinckneya bracteata	fever tree (PC)
Prunus americana	wild plum (MPC)
Prunus serotina	black cherry (MPC)
Styrax americanus	American silverbell (MPC)
Vaccinium arboreum	huckleberry (MPC)
Viburnum prunifolium	blackhaw viburnum (MPC)

POPULAR SPRING-BLOOMING EXOTIC SHRUBS

Camellia japonica	camellia
Forsythia spp.	forsythia
Rhododendron (southern indica hybrids)	southern indica azalea
Rhododendron ponticum	Kurume azalea
Spiraea japonica	Japanese spiraea (inv.)
Syringa spp.	lilac
Weigela spp.	weigela

Suggested Native Substitutes for Popular Nonnative (Exotic) Plants (continued)

Aesculus pavia	red buckeye (PC)
Amorpha fruticosa	indigo bush (MPC)
Aronia arbutifolia	red chokeberry (MPC)
Aronia melanocarpa	black chokeberry (MP)
Ceanothus americanus	New Jersey tea (MPC)
Cliftonia monophylla	buckwheat tree (PC)
Crataegus phaenopyrum	Washington hawthorn (MPC)
Fothergilla gardenii	coastal witch alder (C)
Fothergilla latifolia	witch alder (MP)
Hamamelis virginiana	witch hazel (MPC)
Hydrangea quercifolia	oakleaf hydrangea (MPC)
Itea virginica	Virginia sweet spire (MPC)
Lindera benzoin	spicebush (MPC)
Prunus angustifolia	Chickasaw plum (PC)
Rhododendron arborescens	sweet azalea (MPC)
Rhododendron atlanticum	coastal azalea (C)
Rhododendron austrinum	Florida flame azalea (MPC)
Rhododendron calendulaceum	flame azalea (MP)
Rhododendron canescens	honeysuckle azalea (MPC)
Rhododendron periclymenoides	pinxter bloom azalea (MPC)
Rhododendron viscosum	swamp azalea (MPC)
Stewartia malacodendron	silky camellia (MPC)
Viburnum dentatum	arrowwood viburnum (MPC)
Viburnum nudum	smooth withe rod (MPC)

POPULAR SUMMER-BLOOMING EXOTIC SHRUBS

Buddleia davidii (nonsterile, invasive)	butterfly bush (inv.)
Hydrangea spp.	hydrangea (exotic varieties)

Nerium oleander	oleander (inv.)
Rosa 'Knock Out'	Knock Out rose
Rosa multiflora	multiflora rose (inv.)

SUGGESTED NATIVE SUBSTITUTES

Aesculus parviflora	bottlebrush buckeye (MPC)
Amorpha fruticosa	indigo bush (MPC)
Buddleia (sterile cultivars, noninvasive)	butterfly bush (sterile cultivars) (MPC)
Cephalanthus occidentalis	buttonbush (MPC)
Clethra acuminata	mountain pepperbush (MP)
Clethra alnifolia	summersweet (MPC)
Diervilla sessilifolia	southern bush honeysuckle (M)
Erythrina herbacea	coral bean (C)
Hibiscus coccineus	scarlet rose mallow (PC)
Hibiscus moscheutos	rose mallow (MPC)
Hydrangea arborescens	wild hydrangea (MPC)
Hydrangea radiata	silverleaf hydrangea (MP)
Philadelphus inodorus	Appalachian mock orange (MPC)
Physocarpus opulifolius	ninebark (MP)
Rhododendron catawbiense	catawba rhododendron (MP)
Rhododendron maximum	rosebay rhododendron (MP)
Spiraea tomentosa	steeplebush spiraea (MPC)

POPULAR SUMMER-BLOOMING EXOTIC TREES

| Lagerstroemia indica | crape myrtle |

SUGGESTED NATIVE SUBSTITUTES

Aesculus flava	yellow buckeye (MP)
Catalpa bignonoides	southern catalpa (MPC)
Cladrastis kentukea	yellowwood (MP)
Cotinus obovatus	American smoke tree (MPC)
Cyrilla racemiflora	titi (PC)
Franklinia alatamaha	franklinia (MPC)

Suggested Native Substitutes for Popular Nonnative (Exotic) Plants (continued)

Gordonia lasianthus	loblolly bay (C)
Kalmia latifolia	mountain laurel (MP)
Magnolia grandiflora	southern magnolia (PC)
Oxydendrum arboreum	sourwood (MPC)

INVASIVE EXOTIC VINES

Ampelopsis brevipedunculata	porcelain berry vine (inv.)
Celastrus orbiculatus	oriental bittersweet (inv.)
Clematis terniflora	sweet autumn clematis (inv.)
Hedera helix	English ivy (inv.)
Ipomoea quamoclit	cypress vine (inv.)
Lonicera japonica	Japanese honeysuckle (inv.)
Wisteria floribunda	Japanese wisteria (inv.)
Wisteria sinensis	Chinese wisteria (inv.)

SUGGESTED NATIVE SUBSTITUTES

Ampelaster carolinianus	climbing aster (PC)
Aristolochia macrophylla	Dutchman's-pipe vine (MPC)
Bignonia capreolata	cross vine (MPC)
Campsis radicans	trumpet creeper (MPC)
Clematis virginiana	virgin's bower (MPC)
Gelsemium sempervirens	Carolina jessamine (MPC)
Hydrangea barbara	climbing hydrangea (MPC)
Lonicera sempervirens	coral honeysuckle (MPC)
Parthenocissus quinquefolia	Virginia creeper (MPC)
Passiflora incarnata	passionflower vine (MPC)
Vitis rotundifolia	muscadine grape vine (MPC)
Wisteria frutescens	American wisteria (PC)

INVASIVE EXOTIC GROUND COVERS

Hedera helix	English ivy (inv.)
Liriope spicata	monkey grass (inv.)

Vinca major	bigleaf periwinkle (inv.)
Vinca minor	common periwinkle (inv.)

SUGGESTED NATIVE SUBSTITUTES

Asarum arifolium	heartleaf ginger (MPC)
Berberis repens	creeping mahonia (MPC)
Calyptocarpus vialis	straggler daisy (MPC)
Chrysogonum virginianum	green-and-gold (MPC)
Gaultheria procumbens	American wintergreen (MPC)
Heuchera americana	American alumroot (MPC)
Juniperus communis var. depressa	ground juniper (MP)
Mitchella repens	partridgeberry (MPC)
Onoclea sensibilis	sensitive fern (MPC)
Pachysandra procumbens	Allegheny spurge (MPC)
Phlox nivalis	trailing phlox (MPC)
Polystichum acrostichoides	Christmas fern (MPC)
Vaccinium crassifolium	creeping blueberry (PC)
Veronica repens	creeping speedwell (MPC)
Woodwardia areolata	netted chain fern (MPC)
Xanthorhiza simplicissima	yellowroot (MPC)
Zamia integrifolia	coontie (C)

INVASIVE EXOTIC ORNAMENTAL GRASSES

Arundo donax	giant reed grass (inv.)
Cortaderia selloana	pampas grass (inv.)
Imperata cylindrica	Japanese blood grass (inv.)
Miscanthus sinensis	Chinese silver grass (inv.)
Miscanthus sacchariflorus	Japanese silver grass (inv.)
Pennisetum setaceum	fountain grass (inv.)
Phyllostachys aurea	golden bamboo (inv.)

SUGGESTED NATIVE SUBSTITUTES

Andropogon gerardii	big bluestem (MPC)
Andropogon glomeratus	bushy bluestem (MPC)

Suggested Native Substitutes for Popular Nonnative (Exotic) Plants (continued)

Andropogon ternarius	splitbeard bluestem (MPC)
Andropogon virginicus	broom sedge (MPC)
Chasmanthium latifolium	northern sea oats (MPC)
Deschampsia cespitosa	tufted hair grass (MPC)
Elymus hystrix	bottlebrush grass (MP)
Eragrostis spectabilis	purple love grass (MPC)
Muhlenbergia capillaris	pink muhly grass (MPC)
Muhlenbergia sericea	purple muhly grass (C)
Panicum amarum	bitter panic grass (C)
Panicum virgatum	switch grass (MPC)
Rhyncospora latifolia	white-topped sedge (C)
Saccharum giganteum	sugarcane plume grass (MPC)
Sorghastrum nutans	yellow Indian grass (MPC)
Tridens flavus	purpletop grass (MPC)

INVASIVE EXOTIC PERENNIALS

Chrysanthemum leucanthemum	oxeye daisy (inv.)
Daucus carota	Queen Anne's lace (inv.)
Lantana camara	common lantana (inv.)
Lythrum salicaria	purple loosestrife (inv.)

SUGGESTED NATIVE SUBSTITUTES

Any native full-sun perennial

INDEX